Jan Harkopf

Investment Criteria for Mutual Fund Selection

Anchor Academic
Publishing

Harkopf, Jan: Investment Criteria for Mutual Fund Selection, Hamburg, Anchor
Academic Publishing 2016

Buch-ISBN: 978-3-96067-076-6
PDF-eBook-ISBN: 978-3-96067-576-1
Druck/Herstellung: Anchor Academic Publishing, Hamburg, 2016

Bibliografische Information der Deutschen Nationalbibliothek:
Die Deutsche Nationalbibliothek verzeichnet diese Publikation in der Deutschen
Nationalbibliografie; detaillierte bibliografische Daten sind im Internet über
http://dnb.d-nb.de abrufbar.

Bibliographical Information of the German National Library:
The German National Library lists this publication in the German National Bibliography.
Detailed bibliographic data can be found at: http://dnb.d-nb.de

© Anchor Academic Publishing, Imprint der Diplomica Verlag GmbH
Hermannstal 119k, 22119 Hamburg
http://www.diplomica-verlag.de, Hamburg 2016
Printed in Germany

Contents

Abbreviations

APM	Adverse price movement
AuM	Assets under management
BaFin	*(Bundesanstalt für Finanzdienstleistungsaufsicht)*
	Federal Financial Supervisory Authority
ETF	Exchange traded fund
IPO	Initial public offering
MBA	Master business administration
SAT	Scholastic assessment test
SEC	Security and Exchange Commission
SEO	Seasoned equity offerings
UK	United Kingdom
US	United States
USA	United States of America

Symbols

α_{fund}	(Alpha) Outperformance of mutual fund to the benchmark index
β_{fund}	(Beta) Mutual fund sensibility of co movement to the benchmark index
$\varepsilon_{fund,t}$	(Epsilon) Error term of regression
$R_{f,t}$	Return on a risk free security
$R_{fund,t}$	Return on a mutual fund
$R_{index,t}$	Return on a benchmark index
$w_{fund,i}$	Weights of asset i in the fund
$w_{index,i}$	Weights of asset i in the benchmark index

Figures

1   Introduction

1.1   Investments in Mutual Funds

The assets under management (AuM) invested in mutual funds worldwide amount to $26.8 trillion at the end of 2012. Approximately 50% of these assets are invested in the United States (US), followed by Europe with 30%.[1] The importance of mutual funds for individual investors in general has increased in recent decades. This becomes apparent when looking at the increased share of households owning mutual funds within individual retirement plans and defined contribution plans. Younger households in the US tend also to participate stronger in mutual funds,[2] which implies that these retail investors are holding investments over longer periods and might even have larger invested stakes in mutual funds. I assume this pattern to apply to the European market, as well. In Germany, over 50% of assets in mutual funds are hold by individual investors at the end of 2008. This number has decreased from around 70% in 2005.[3] I further assume that this decrease is a consequence of the financial crisis, since individual investors are more likely to follow a general market climate than investing when markets are down.[4]

The main purpose of mutual fund investors is usually receiving a return which is above or at least close to the mutual fund's benchmark.[5] Consequently investors want identify and invest in those mutual funds which show these patterns in the future. Some mutual funds get much on attention since they generate extraordinary high performance; examples for these mutual funds are the Fidelity Magellan fund or the Schroder Ultra Fund. The last mentioned fund yields a performance of 107% annually in the time period of 1999 to 2001.[6] But the question when looking at these mutual funds is: Is it possible to predict such performance before funds exhibit such outstanding performance? Recent studies outlined in foot note 7 below showed strong doubts whether this is possible, since mutual fund performance, at least in the short run, is rather a random walk than a result of managerial skill.[7] Academics go even further while stating that active managed mutual funds on average underperform their

---

[1] Cf. ICI Factbook (2013) p. 25.
[2] Cf. ICI Factbook (2013) p.116.
[3] Cf. Jank (2010) p. 8.
[4] Cf. Celati (2004) p. 66.
[5] Cf. Barras/Scaillet/Wermers (2010) p. 183.
[6] Cf. Kosowski, et al. (2006) p. 2551.
[7] Cf. Barras/Scaillet/Wermers (2010) p. 180; Fama/French (2010) p. 1916; Kosowski, et al. (2006) p. 2554.

corresponding benchmark by the costs in expenses.[8] Furthermore, there is some evidence that the proportion of unskilled managers have increased in recent years while the proportion of skilled managers have diminished. [9] This finding makes it harder to "identify" those mutual funds managed by skilled executives.

In the past, mutual fund investors focused extensively on performance or performance linked patterns, like the Morningstar star rating and thus chased intensively past performance.[10] This seems somewhat surprising since performance persists only over short horizons and is also more persistent for weak mutual funds (1 und 2 star rated) than well performing mutual funds since the distinction between average and top performing funds is hardly possible.[11] Thus chasing past performance seems to be a rather inferior strategy.

Consequently investors should have some interest to identify alternative tools, which show a high correlation to future mutual fund performance. One of these tools could be the 2004 introduced Morningstar Stewardship rating for mutual funds, which provides investors with information about some governance related issues of mutual funds. [12] This might be of special interest for investors since some unfavorable patterns of many mutual funds are partly the result of weak governance, i.e. a weak alignment of investors' and managers' interests. In many cases such patterns result in an inferior performance.[13] A working paper published in 2008 suggests that investors seem to react on the Morningstar Stewardship rating by redeeming or purchasing mutual fund shares.[14]

---

[8] Cf. Fama/French (2010) p. 1941.

[9] Cf. Barras/Scaillet/Wermers (2010) p. 199.

[10] Cf. Del Guercio/Tkac (2001) p.37; Del Guercio/Tkac (2008) p. 918.

[11] Cf. Blake/Morey (2000) p. 467.; Brown/Goetzmann (1995) p. 691 - 693; Carhart (1993) p. 57; Hendricks/Patel/Zeckhauser (1993) p. 93.

[12] Cf. Morningstar Inc. (2010b) p. 1; Wellman/Zhou (2008) p.1.

[13] Cf. Weak alignment of investors and mutual fund managers may be the result of various reasons. For example management and board link pattern, but as well patterns linked to the mutual fund itself like the affiliation to a bank or if the mutual fund is public hold or private hold.

[14] Cf. Wellman/Zhou (2008) p.1.

1.2   Remarks and Structure of the Study

This study focuses on open end mutual funds and do not look at closed end mutual funds, since closed end mutual funds are much less common and have some different characteristics. Additionally I focus mainly on actively managed mutual funds, as these funds are more common[15] and also show more prosperities than passive mutual funds. Nevertheless, when analyzing some aspects I will look at passive mutual funds, since it is easier to infer on investors' behavior. This is due to the fact that some active mutual fund attributes blur some effects and behavior pattern.

It should be noted that the vast majority of literature in this study are based on works relating to the US market, other markets are only considered partly. Thus when adopting these results, those results linked to regulatory constraints and requirements might be misleading in particular. Nevertheless, the basic statements should be valid for markets outside the US as well, especially those linked to the behavior pattern and incentives.

The study is structured as follows:

- In chapter two I give a short overview about the economics and both advantages and disadvantages of mutual funds.
- In chapter three I focus on mutual fund performance and raise the question of the purpose and usefulness of active investments. Based on that I ask whether performance is persistent and what the determinants of mutual fund flows are.
- In chapter four I will analyze mutual funds in general and also focus on some influence factors on its performance. Some points in this chapter are of rather theoretic nature.
- In chapter five I will introduce some alternative measures and will also explain which of the aforementioned attributes or methods should be used or rather avoided when selecting mutual funds.
- In chapter six I will conclude the results and will and briefly address open questions.

---

[15] The share of closed end funds for the US amounts less than 2% at the end of 2012. See ICI Factbook (2013) p. 2 (front cover).

2 Mutual Funds

2.1 Mutual Fund Basics

2.1.1 Overview and Economies

Open end mutual funds could be distinguished in different ways. Important distinctions are active or passive managed mutual funds. Passive mutual funds or index mutual funds are used to be "replicating the return on an index with a strategy of buying and holding all (or almost all) index stocks in the official index proportions"[16] with relative low costs.[17] When extending index funds to Exchange traded funds (ETFs), the definition above is no more valid, since sometimes those funds are swap-based with the result that the assets in the portfolios of these funds are sometimes totally uncorrelated to the index mirrored.[18] By assuming that markets are efficient and thus generating outperformance in active investments is nearly impossible, investments in passive funds might be considered to be rational. Further reasons are that these funds do not trade actively and consequently save costs for research and active trading.[19] Passive mutual funds are commonly associated with ETFs, whereas lots of "classic" mutual funds are also tradable on exchange, though they are no ETFs.[20, 21] An active investment is more complicated to specify, basically it can be "defined as any deviation from passive management"[22], respective benchmark index or strategy. Furthermore, mutual funds differ by the assets they are invested in (e.g. equity, bonds, mutual funds, etc.).

Alongside the increased importance of mutual funds for individual investors, funds are also used by institutional investors. Increasing institutional holdings in mutual funds show some important signals which may be partly supportive for retail investors when selecting mutual funds.[23]

Mutual fund markets around the world show partly different characteristics. The US market for example is different to the rest of the world in regard of the average fund size. US funds are on average five times bigger than European funds and 17 times bigger than Asian funds.[24]

---

[16] Cremers/Petajisto (2009) p. 3334.
[17] Cf. Fama/French (2010) p. 1915 f., 1922.
[18] Cf. Heidorn/Winker/Löw (2010) p. 7.
[19] Cf. Malkiel (2010) p. 119.
[20] Cf. Heidorn/Winker/Löw (2010) p. 7.
[21] ETFs are unique due to a so called "in kind process", which causes that each investor carry the costs of redeeming or purchasing fund shares. See: Huang/Guedj (2009) p. 2.
[22] Cremers/Petajisto (2009) p. 3334.
[23] Cf. Chung/Zhang (2011) p. 254; Evans/Fahlenbrach (2012) p. 3530, Matsumura/Shin (2005) p. 107.
[24] Cf. Ferreira et al. (2013) p. 488.

The existence of economies of scale and economies of scope in mutual funds are broadly discussed in literature, but the results are diverse.[25] This can be argued by different sources of such economies, which are sometimes supportive or obstructive to these economies and these effects differ over diverse markets and different funds. Economies or diseconomies of scale are influenced by many sources and thus the over-all impact is not clear, since the single effects might be weighted out. Looking briefly at the economies of scale they seem to be common features for the mutual funds AuM outside the USA and for international invested funds located in the USA. In contrast, domestic funds in the USA show diseconomies of scale. The diseconomies of scale in the USA are explained by liquidity constrains. This finding persists even when control-ling for the size of US funds, which seems irritating because the US stock market is more developed in comparison to other markets.[26] These conclusions are especially im-portant because most of the mutual fund studies are located in the US. Thus interpreting this finding as common feature for mutual funds worldwide might cause a bias.

Additionally, increasing AuM leads to adverse price movements, when buying or selling the underlying stocks. This effect especially applies when the mutual fund is becoming larger or when the fund is investing in smaller markets or less liquid stocks. The increasing size also causes the problem that mutual funds are getting less flexible compared to smaller funds when shifting portfolio holdings quickly. In addition, mutual funds tend to scale their portfolio, meaning that they primarily increase their holdings in those stocks they are already invested in, instead of searching for alternatives. Investments in alternatives only take place when the costs of the current investments are getting too high. This results in the fact that the diversifications of larger mutual funds are only marginal higher than those of smaller ones.[27]

The evidence of economies of scale and economies of scope on the fund family level is much clearer. It can be explained due to savings in back office and market research costs, since these costs are divided over a broader base.[28] Fund families usually run different mutual funds which are invested in the same stocks or at least in the same market. At the same time the essential research costs do not increase proportionally with AuM and are not affected by increased trading sizes. The same is true for the back office costs, because ordinary supervisory costs do not increase to the same extent as

---

[25] See for example: Cf. Yan, X. ((2008); Chen et al. (2004).
[26] Cf. Ferreira et al. (2013) p. 483, 488.
[27] Cf. Chen et al. (2004) p. 1276ff., Pollet/Wilson (2008) p.2941 f., 2944.
[28] Cf. Yan, X. ((2008) p. 760.

AuM increases. It is argued further that larger fund families are able to receive better concessions on trading commissions.[29] Limits in economies of scale are induced due to hierarchies which are commonly associated with larger funds, because managers have to explain their decisions and investment strategies they want to implement.[30]

2.1.2 Advantages and Disadvantages of Mutual Funds

The main advantages of investments in mutual funds are portfolio diversification, a professional asset management, liquidity and usually an overall equity structure. The diversification yields in a decrease of unsystematic risk, which individual investors can hardly receive by investing their assets in single stocks. The professional portfolio management is important, because individuals are usually unable to scan the entire market and identify "good" investing opportunities. Liquidity is related to the fact that investors can buy and redeem fund shares on a daily basis.[31] These advantages count especially for less wealthy individual investors, who cannot afford a professional portfolio manager or investing their assets diversified on their own.

However, mutual funds show some drawbacks. For example only a few (if any) active mutual funds are able to outperform their benchmark after costs. Even before costs are deducted the picture is only slightly better.[32] This raises the question if investments in active mutual funds are reasonable, since on the long run such investments seem to be a zero sum or even a losing game.

Beside this, especially in mutual funds affiliated to banking conglomerates or publicly hold mutual fund families, the conflicts of interest hypothesis play an important role and cause or may cause some serious problems. The conflicts of interest hypothesis is not clearly defined but it can be summarized as a situation in which one party can take a gain by actions harmful for the counterparty. Such actions require information asymmetries. Consequently given a situation in which both parties are equally informed, nobody can take advantages of these actions.[33] In our case the mutual fund manager respective the financial institution has superior information against the mutual fund investors. The conflict of interests in mutual funds may result for example in unfavorable features like a lack of disclosure to investors, tax inefficiency and

---

[29] Cf. Chen et al. (2004) p. 1278.
[30] Cf. Chen et al. (2004) p. 1278f.; Ferreira et al. (2013) p. 518.
[31] Cf. Ciccotello (2010) p. 5 ff.; Smith, (2010a) p.38 ff..
[32] Cf. Fama/French (2010) p. 1923, 1941; Ferreira et al. (2013) p. 485,493,518, Smith, (2010a) p.40.
[33] Cf. Mehran/Stulz (2007) p. 267 - 269.

inadequate high fees and loads, window dressing and other questionable actions.[34] Some of these actions became apparent in the scandals in the early 2000s. During those scandals mutual funds allowed some investors to use abusive and partly illegal market timing or late trading. The "costs" of these actions were mainly borne by buy-and-hold investors,[35] such as retail investors holding mutual funds in their individual retirement plans. Interestingly the participants in this scandal are mainly big players with nearly 20% or $1.2 trillion out of $7.2 trillion in long term assets und management.[36] Such a situation does not necessary cause drawbacks for investors. In some situations investors might even take profits from this superior information.[37]

2.2   Mutual Fund Functionality

This chapter will present a brief overview about the functionality of mutual funds. These are commonly organized as corporation or trust. They are supervised by a board of inside and outside directors. Outside directors might have diverse backgrounds and their number should amount for least 75% of the board members. Outside directors are at least theoretically independent and should strengthen the power of the board and should protect investors' rights as "independent watchdogs".[38] The board of directors appoints the investment advisors respective the managers running the operative business, who are commonly employed by an advisory firm. In addition, the board also negotiates the fee with the advisory firm to be charged to the investors in the fund.[39,40]

Mutual funds are created by mutual fund companies. After funds were initialized, mutual funds provide seed money and operate outside the market for instance. After a period of approximately 6 months the fund is opened for sale to investors. The return history of this period is usually reported only, if the fund has performed well.[41] In the day to day business, sell and purchase orders for fund shares are collected by the fund and executed at the end of the trading day.[42] This characteristic is advantageous for the

---

[34] Cf. Adams/Mansi/Nishikawa (2012) p. 2245; Kacperczyk/Sialm/Zheng (2006) p. 2379; Smith, (2010a) p.40 ff..

[35] Cf. McCabe (2009) p. 1.

[36] Cf. Bogle, J. C. (2010) p. 283.

[37] Mutual funds affiliated to credit bank usually profit from this relationship, see Massa/Rehman (2008) p.288 ff. and chapter 4.5.3.

[38] Cf. Chen/Huang (2011) p. 312; Ciccotello (2010) p. 4 ff.; SEC (1999) p. 2.

[39] Cf. Ding/Wermers (2012) p. 6; Mehran/Stulz (2007) p. 271.

[40] When a mutual fund is initiated the investment advisory firm is only shareholder, consequently he is able to chose the "first" set of board members, see Kuhnen (2009) p. 2186. The conflict of interest resulting on this structure is discussed in chapter 4.3.2.

[41] Cf. Fama/French (2010) p. 1923f..

[42] Cf. Huang/Guedj (2009) p. 2.

mutual fund. By collecting shares, the fund trades less because purchasing and selling orders might be weighting out each other on a daily basis. Mutual funds must be able to redeem and sell their share from investors at the net asset value every day. This structure is called "self-liquidating". The feature requires the fund to hold some cash, or at least highly liquid assets, which causes the so called cash-drag and can erode performance.[43] The above described lagged structure brings some drawbacks for investors because the price of the mutual fund might have dropped within that day. This characteristic has arisen with the increasing importance of online banking and the broad availability of ETFs, which are virtually tradable at any second at market prices. On the other hand "classic" mutual funds are also tradable at exchanges, without meeting the characteristics' of ETFs and therefore do not cause this process.

Mutual funds usually charge fees and expenses to their investors. Fees can be distinguished between front-end load fee, back-end load fee[44] and operating expenses.[45] These costs vary across the globe and the different funds[46]. The front-end load fee is a one-time upfront fee which is charged from investors when buying new shares. The fee represents the costs for the fund associated with buying new stocks and ensures that the existing investors are unharmed by the newly arrived money. The charge also contains remunerations for financial intermediaries to sale shares to private investors. The back-end load fees are charged when selling mutual funds. They cover the costs of selling the underlying assets and should ensure that the remaining investors are unaffected of these trades. Sometimes the back-end load fees are related to the invested amount and the holding period and thus giving incentives for increased holding periods because the cost of redeeming funds becomes lower when the holding period increases.[47] Problems with this structure are that investors in the fund have to bear the price impact of asset inflows and outflows. Some mutual funds introduce back-end fees to lower this impact.[48] The ongoing expenses are covering the operational costs of mutual funds, such as the management fee and other operative costs which include marketing expenses, employee salaries and so on. They are charged on a daily basis as expense ratio based on net asset value.[49]

---

[43] Cf. Ciccotello (2010) p. 5; Heidorn/Winkler/Löw (2010) p.10.
[44] Synonyms for example are: redemption fee, redemption load, rear load, deferred load.
[45] The cost compoinents may separated differently.
[46] Cf. Khorana/Servaes/Tufano (2007) p. 1279.
[47] Cf. Bechmann/Rangvid (2007) p. 667 f., Smith (2010b) p.52 f..
[48] Cf. Bollen (2007) p. 687.
[49] Cf. Iannotta/Navone (2012) p. 847.

2.3 Mutual Fund Ratings

2.3.1 Basics of Mutual Fund Ratings

Two common types of ratings are fund ratings and credit ratings. These two types show very important distinctions. While a credit rating is forward looking and measures an absolute default risk, fund ratings are commonly only backward looking and measure the past performance relative to funds in a peer group and do not incorporate qualitative facts.[50] In recent times some agencies extended or provided ratings with non-performance factors.[51] There are a few independent rating agencies rating mutual funds around the globe, the most influential one in the USA is Morningstar offering the "star rating".[52] However, there are many more agencies rating mutual funds like Standard & Poors, Feri, Lipper, Euro Fondsnote and Stiftung Warentest.[53] Conceptually (mutual fund) ratings should provide unbiased, new and useful information to market participants to help investors to allocate their assets.[54] Most mutual fund rating agencies represent the results in a simplified score. Morningstar for example provide stars. Especially naive investors tend to rely strongly on such heavily condensed ratings, since retail investors are usually not able to scan the wide range of investment opportunities mutual funds are offering. Rating agencies like Morningstar claim that investors should use the rating only as a starting point and thus not rely solely on the star rating.[55] But the empirical evidence, above all the US market, shows a different picture. The data shows that changes in ratings cause immediate statistically significant market reactions.[56] The European market (e.g. Germany and Finland) presents a different picture. The overall market reaction is lagged and is much weaker.[57] The effect of changes in ratings depends on various reasons like affiliation of investment funds and banks, the usage of ratings for advertising purposes and maybe a less developed mutual fund market.[58]

2.3.2 The Star Rating

Since the Morningstar "star rating" is the most influential mutual fund rating the most literature refers to, it is outlined briefly below. This rating analyses funds and assigns

---

[50] Cf. Hereil et al. (2010) p. 6 - 7.
[51] Cf. Morningstar Inc. (2010b).
[52] Cf. Morningstar Inc. (2010a); Carhart (1997) p. 66.
[53] Cf. Meinhardt (2011) p. 1; Füss et al. (2010) p. 76.
[54] Cf. Del Guercio/Tkac (2008) p. 909, 912; Terraza/Toque (2009) p. 149.
[55] Cf. Füss et al. (2010) p. 76, Morningstar Inc. (2010a) p.1; Russel (2006) p. 85.
[56] Cf. Del Guercio/Tkac (2008) p. 907, 918.
[57] Cf. Füss et al. (2010) p. 83 ff..
[58] Cf. Bessler/Drobetz/Zimmermann (2009) p. 287; Del Guercio/Tkac (2008) p.925; Gerrans, P. (2006) p. 605 f.; Jank (2010) p. 3,6,13 f.,14,18; Russel (2006) p. 85.

one to five stars based on past performance. A five star rating represents the highest score and one star the lowest. The rating scale builds on a normal distribution. The top 10% of funds receive five stars, the next 22.5% receive four stars, and the following 35% of funds from the medium segment and are rated with three stars. The next 22.5% receives two stars and for the bottom 10% one star is assigned. The costs associated with buying and selling mutual funds are deducted. The ongoing expenses are only indirectly incorporated, since they are deducted from the returns. Furthermore the star rating bases on three different time horizons. Time horizons and the weights for each horizon are defined as follows:

Weights of the Morningstar rating

Age of fund	Overall rating
At least three years, but less than five	100% three-year rating
At least five years, but less than 10	60% five-year rating 40% three-year rating
At least 10 years	50% 10-year rating 30% five-year rating 20% three-year rating

Illustration 1: Weights of the Morningstar rating.[59]

Funds younger than 3 years are not included in the rating. The fund's rating bases on the Morningstar's categories defined for different markets and assets where funds are invested in. 2002 the star rating has been changed, since the rating was biased by funds invested in extraordinary well performing industries, Morningstar introduces new and more detailed categories to solve this (potential) drawback. The Morningstar risk adjusted returns now base on an extended expected utility theory.[60] In earlier periods Morningstar has defined risk by a bilinear utility function.[61] Risk was defined as underperformance to the 90 day treasury-bill. When the treasury bill was outperformed the mutual fund has been classified as "riskless". The expected utility theory states that investors are more averse against a potential loss than a potential positive outcome and that investors are willing to give up some assets for a certain yield.[62]

Additionally, since 2004 Morningstar provides a Stewardship Rating. It was introduced after the scandals in the early 2000s and should allow investors identifying well and poorly managed mutual funds.[63]

---

[59] Cf. Morningstar Inc. (2010a).
[60] Cf. Del Guercio/Tkac (2008) p.927; Morningstar Inc. (2010a).
[61] Cf. Sharpe (1998) p. 21.
[62] Cf. Kahneman/Tversky (1979) p. 279; Lisi/Caporin (2009) p. 5; Morningstar Inc. (2006); Morningstar Inc. (2010a).
[63] Cf. Morningstar Inc. (2010b) p. 1; Phillips/Kaplan (2010) p. 171.

3   Mutual Fund Performance

3.1   *What is Important about Mutual Fund Performance*

Ratings mainly based on performance and fund performance itself are the dominant investment criteria when looking at mutual funds. Especially the influence of the star rating becomes apparent when observing the market reactions following changes in Morningstar fund ratings in the USA.[64, 65] When looking at the mutual fund literatures regarding the performance of mutual funds, three main scopes are important:

- Are mutual fund managers able to outperform their benchmark by generating a true alpha? In other words: Are mutual fund managers really skilled? The empirical evidence shows that skill seems to be a scare source and that the short run performance is mainly derived by luck, good luck as well as bad luck.[66]

- The next scope is predictability and persistence in mutual fund performance. This is obviously difficult since performance is used to predict performance and performance is at least partly a random walk.[67] Furthermore, performance persistence is rather a short run phenomenon and is rather a result compared with worse performing mutual funds.[68]

- Mutual fund flows are of special interest, since both the fund's performance influences the asset flows in and out of funds and the flows influence the performance and vice versa. The performance directly influences the fund flows, as investors chase past performance.[69] Inflows on the other hand lead to increasing assets under management and the funds face decreasing economies of scale.[70]

3.2   *Active Investments*

3.2.1   Why Using Active Strategies?

Investors use active investment strategies to outperforming a corresponding passive alternative. Otherwise it would be rational to invest the assets in passive strategies like an ETF, which yields the benchmark return minus marginal costs for "sure", without the

---

[64] Cf. Del Guercio/Tkac (2001) p. 37; Del Guercio/Tkac (2008) p. 918; Knuutila/Puttonen/Smythe (2007) p. 89.
[65] See chapter 3.4 for a more detailed discussion
[66] Barras/Scaillet/Wermers (2010) p. 179 ff.; Fama/French (2010) p. 1919 f.; Kosowski, et al. (2006) p. 2551 - 2555.
[67] Cf. Barras/Scaillet/Wermers (2010) p. 180; Fama/French (2010) p. 1916; Kosowski, et al. (2006) p. 2554.
[68] Cf. Hendricks/Patel/Zeckhauser (1993) p. 93.
[69] Cf. Del Guercio/Tkac (2001) p.37; Del Guercio/Tkac (2008) p.918.
[70] Cf. Blake/Morey (2000) p. 467.

risk of underperforming the benchmark substantially.[71] Due to the fact that stocks in active mutual funds are traded actively and thus have other weights than the benchmark, they may show higher risks than their passive counterparts. Furthermore, active mutual funds charge higher fees on the expense of their investors to remunerate managerial skill, research costs and higher trading costs.[72] Unfortunately studies show that at least on average outperforming passive strategies is hardly possible[73] or even impossible as on average a negative alpha indicates.[74, 75] Investors are going to anticipate the inability to receive excess returns (in the long run) and now only want to collect at least the return of the passive benchmark (alpha equals zero).[76]

3.2.2 Skill in the Mutual Fund Industry

Assuming fairly efficient markets it seems apparent that mutual fund managers need skill or superior information to outperform the market. Otherwise no rational investor would put any money in an active mutual fund, since it would be a zero sum or even a losing game.[77] Skill can be defined either as the managers' ability to generate a true positive alpha after costs or a true positive alpha before costs. The second definition might be justifiable since the expenses charged are not essentially linked to the management itself.[78] But nevertheless investors only receive net returns, thus the second definition is rather a theoretical one. Skill is derived either due to stock picking ability or market timing ability, whereas stock picking ability may be simply linked to superior information, provided by managers of firms the fund is invested in.[79] Based on the assumption above, skill would be expressed in two different ways, increasing the return of a portfolio or minimizing the "insurable risk" and so increase risk adjusted returns.[80] This is important since investors usually show some risk aversion and thus prefer less risky investments instead of risky ones when yielding the same expected return.[81] The

---

[71] Some ETFs have a total expense ratio of 0.15% p.a. or below. The bid-ask spread, expressed by the Xetra liquidity measure of some ETFs is around 10 basis points when buying and selling €100,000 at the same time. (Deutsche Börse AG (2013) p.4).

[72] Carhart (1997) p.66.

[73] Cf. Barras/Scaillet/Wermers (2010) p. 179 ff.; Fama/French (2010) p. 1919 f.; Kosowski, et al. (2006) p.2551 - 2555.

[74] Cf. Barras/Scaillet/Wermers (2010) p. 199.

[75] Alpha is constantly negative since 1996 until the end of the study in 2006, where alpha amounts minus one. See Barras/Scaillet/Wermers (2010) p. 199.

[76] Cf. Berk/Green (2004) p. 1271.

[77] Cf. Antypas, et al. (2009) p. 2; Ferson/Schadt (1996) p. 426.

[78] Cf. Barras/Scaillet/Wermers (2010) p.209.

[79] Cf. Bodson/Cavenaile/Sougné (2013) p. 96; Cohen/Frazzini/Malloy (2008) p. 951 f., 954.

[80] Cf. Jensen, M. C. (1968) p. 389.

[81] Cf. Jensen (1968) p. 389; Tversky/Kahneman (1992) p. 297f..

risk aversion applies as long as the probability of the outcome is not extremely unlikely, which gives investors incentives for gambling.[82] Skill would be expressed in the managers' ability to "predict" the return of the market or the return of individual stocks. In addition to the "pure" skill the manager should be able to enforce her strategy within the fund and should also be willing to invest in the stocks of whom she believes (knows) that they will outperform the market.[83] Otherwise a managerial skill would be useless.

Consequently, investors have some interest in knowing whether the manager respective the management team is skilled and courageous to follow the strategy described in the prospectus, resulting ideally in outperforming the market. In this context it is also important that the management is aware of some behavior pattern like the disposition effect. Mutual funds which are prone to disposition and do not implement suitable actions might unintended change the investment style.[84]

Identifying true alpha funds sounds simple but the main challenge is to differentiate between skilled funds and those who are just lucky. The Fama and French paper "Luck versus Skill" has received some attention[85] and documents like many others that the vast majority of outperformance and underperformance, at least in the short run, is determined by luck.[86] All these studies state in a more or less pessimistic manner that mutual funds on average are unable to outperform the market after costs. These studies do not conclude that managers in general are unable to outperform the market, but skill is blurred away by less or even unskilled managers.[87] The most important finding is that it seems nearly impossible to distinguish between funds run by skilled but unlucky managers and funds run by lucky but unskilled managers, at least when using performance patterns only.[88] Although this conclusion is not new[89] investors are further going on and investing in active managed portfolios, preferable those performing well in the past.

---

[82] Cf. Kahneman/Tversky (1979) p. 265 - 268, 275.
[83] Cf. Jensen (1968) p. 389 f., 395.
[84] Cf. Cici (2012) p. 799.
[85] See for example: Mamudi (2009)
[86] Cf. Barras/Scaillet/Wermers (2010) p.179, 181, 184; Fama/French (2010) p.1915; Kosowski, et al. (2006) p. 2553.
[87] Cf. Kosowski, et al. (2006) p. 2562, 2573.
[88] Cf. Fama/French (2010) p.1933.
[89] Cf. Jensen (1968) p. 389 f..

The fraction of mutual fund managers with stock picking ability is higher in (aggressive) growth oriented funds whereas balanced or income funds tend to show higher fractions of managers with lower or even no stock picking ability. At the same time managers in growth oriented funds do not show persistence in skill which might be linked to the fact that their talent is influenced by decreasing returns to scale.[90] This finding would, at least theoretically, result in a kind of equilibrium state where all mutual funds are endowed with zero alphas, as predicted by Berk and Green in their 2004 published paper.[91]

Looking closer at the recent published studies, three types of mutual funds and mutual fund managers are distinguished, respective.[92]

- **Unskilled managers** are unable to generate a return covering the expenses and the trading costs, resulting in a true negative alpha.

- **Average skilled** managers are able to cover the costs they cause which results in zero alpha.

- **Skilled Managers** are able to cover trading costs and expenses and achieve a surplus resulting in a true a positive alpha.[93]

The percentage of skilled managers or more precisely the percentage of mutual funds that are able to beat the benchmark by skill is becoming smaller over the last decades.[94] In detail the share of skilled managers has declined from roughly 15% in the early 1990s to less than 1% in the mid-2000s. Additionally the share of unskilled managers has risen from roughly 10% to 24% in the same period of time. The share of true zero alpha funds have remained fairly constant at around 75% which reflects the long run predictions of Berk and Green as equilibrium funds.[95] It should be noted that different studies show different numbers in detail since they are based on different methods, time horizons or markets. But the conclusions in these studies regarding the general development are quite similar.[96]

There are some reasons in order to explain this development. The first reason is linked to the efficient market hypothesis and states that markets are getting more efficient over time, whereas the managers' ability stays relatively constant. Consequently the share of

---

[90] Cf. Barras/Scaillet/Wermers (2010) p.181,202;.Kosowski, et al. (2006) p.2555 f..
[91] Cf. Berk/Green (2004) p. 1271.
[92] Some studies assign the skill on the manager level other rather on the mutual fund.
[93] Cf. Barras/Scaillet/Wermers (2010) p.183.
[94] Cf. Barras/Scaillet/Wermers (2010) p.181; Kosowski, et al. (2006) p.2554.
[95] Cf. Barras/Scaillet/Wermers (2010) p. 199.
[96] Cf. Barras/Scaillet/Wermers (2010) p.199; Kosowski, et al. (2006) p.2575 f..

managers who are potentially able to manage outperforming funds is getting smaller. The second explanation states that these highly skilled managers are more willing to work for hedge funds, since mutual funds might limit their managerial abilities by regulatory constraints. Additionally, hedge funds might offer these managers an even higher remuneration.[97] It seems also rational to assume that the growth of the mutual fund market attracts many unskilled managers.[98]

A more intuitive reason for the mentioned development is linked to the fact that all investors on average only can receive the return of the market (passive strategy), if mutual funds on average would outperform the market, other market participants would lose. With an increasing number of mutual funds and a bigger market share invested in mutual funds, outperformance is getting less likely. Moreover, in a situation where investing in mutual funds is a winning game for "sure" no rational investor would invest her assets elsewhere, thus mutual funds would reflect the market, consequently an average outperformance would be impossible. This can even be assumed when more assets are invested in mutual funds.

In addition to that it can be argued that the proportion of skilled managers is higher than the common literature suggests. This notion is based on the fact that fund managers are forced to trade due to liquidity demands of their investors which erodes performance.[99] Assuming an asset turnover of 100%, liquidity induced trading erodes performance by 1.5 to 2% annually.[100] Nevertheless, from the investors' point of view it is basically meaningless where the performance comes from.[101]

3.3 *Persistence in Mutual Fund Performance and Mutual Fund Ratings*

Performance persistence in mutual funds is debated extensively in the literature.[102] Persistence is linked to managerial characteristics and skill, thus a superior manager should be able to generate a persistent positive alpha. Due to the fact that ratings are built strongly on fund performance, conclusions regarding the fund's performance can be derived when looking at ratings. If mutual fund performance persists, mutual funds

---

[97] The number of incentive fee mutual funds amounts around 1.5 to 3 % of total mutual fund markets in the US. See: Elton/Gruber/Blake (2003) p. 781; Madhur (2005) p. 5.

[98] Cf. Fama/French (2010) p.1941; Kosowski, et al. (2006) p.2575.

[99] At this point the disposition effect might play a major role since managers are quite likely to sell winners instead of losers, when they are facing liquidity demand. See: Cici (2012) p. 799.

[100] Edelen (1999) p. 440 f..

[101] A potential solution to this would be, closing the fund for new investors. But this is contradicts with a fee structure based on the assets under management.

[102] See for example: Blake/Morey (2000); Brown/Goetzmann (1995); Carhart (1993); Hendricks/Patel/ Zeckhauser (1993).

investors would be able to use past performance for their investment decisions. Thus investors would rational search for past winners and past losers in order to purchase, redeem or avoid any funds.[103] Given that the short run performance is mostly a random walk, it seems hard to identify persistence and predict the future fund performance solely based on past performance. The results are quite divers because persistence heavily depends on the performance measurement,[104] the market or industry and the period analyzed. In general it is possible to identify the worst performing funds (one star and two stars), whereas there is evidence that the "real" stars are hardly to identify. And not surprisingly, since ratings only use relative measures, they cannot be used as indicator for beating an absolute benchmark.[105]

Ratings are more likely to identify superior individual funds when funds are compared with their close competitors. Whereby this is linked to characteristics like stocks (e. g. small or large cap), the market (e.g. emerging markets or rather matured markets like the US or Europe) and the investment style (e.g. growth or income) the mutual funds invest in. In contrast to compare mutual funds only with their close competitors, comparing funds to a broader base of funds would cause a bias in the rating due to systematic movements of entire industries. In that situation ratings would basically identify only strong or weak performing industries[106] but not superior managed funds within the same industry. This weakness became apparent in the aftermath of the new economy bubble where funds located in the "new economy industries" were rated quite high. After the burst of the new economy bubble, the situation changes abruptly.[107] On the other hand, the predictive power declines,[108] since in that case the results reflect, if at all, the (superior or inferior) fund performance and not industry specific movements. The same study states that performance persistence for the new introduced categories hardly exists.[109]

The persistence of fund ratings based on past performance erodes with increasing time horizons. After one year there are at best 40% of funds rated equally to their initial rating. The highest persistence is observed for the three star rated funds. The tails are characterized by the worst persistence where the percentage declines to roughly 20%.

---

[103] Cf. Brown/Goetzmann (1995) p. 694.
[104] Cf. Casarin et al. (2005) p. 306.
[105] Cf. Antypas, et al. (2009) p. 1; Brown/Goetzmann (1995) p. 680; Blake/Morey (2000) p. 452.
[106] Cf. Casarin et al. (2005) p. 306.
[107] Cf. Kräussl/Sandelowsky (2007) p. 3.
[108] Kräussl/Sandelowsky (2007) p. 1.
[109] Cf. Kräussl/Sandelowsky (2007) p. 3.

One year later the picture darkens even more. Only 10% of funds in the tails still receive the same rating and consequently perform constantly. It is noteworthy that regardless of the rating result at the beginning of the analysis that funds that tend to receive three stars. This probability amounts roughly one third.[110] The likelihood to remain five-star rated after three years has declined to 10% for the European market and to an even lower level for the US and emerging markets. Summarizing these results it could be stated that over a two or three year horizon the initial rating has virtually no or only marginal effect.[111] Consequently the performance has changed in the same way. Interestingly the distribution of the "stars" after three years approximately mirrors the distribution of the stars in the Morningstar rating. This movement is likely to be consistent with "misconceptions on regression", which explain that extra ordinary negative or extraordinary positive outcomes are likely to be followed by an average outcome simply by chance. But people are unaware of this phenomenon or unable to mentally incorporate it and if they discover these tendencies to the mean they assume "spurious causal explanations".[112] This notion is further rational due to the fact that around three fourth of the mutual funds are performing on average in the long haul.[113]

Even older studies like the "hot hands" study by Hendricks, Patel and Zeckhauser published in 1993 lead to similar results. Hot hands are based on a relatively short track of superior performance which usually persists only for one year.[114] Much of the decline in persistence might basically be explained by the findings already mentioned, namely: Past superior performance leads to new flows and thus "a bloated organization and fewer good investment ideas per managed dollar"[115]. Consequently, managers might face decreasing economies of scales in their stock picking skills. In addition there are further arguments which are linked to some behavioral patterns. It is supposed that managers with superior performance are likely to leave the fund for a better opportunity. The fund respective the fund management might be less motivated to continue performing above average since they have received some good reputation and moreover the inflows are likely to remain positive. At the same time investors are reluctant to

---

[110] This pattern reflects the distribution of the star rating, see 2.3.2.
[111] Cf. Hereil et al. (2010) p. 8 - 10.
[112] Cf. Tversky/Kahneman (1974) p. 1126.
[113] Cf. Barras/Scaillet/Wermers (2010) p. 183.
[114] Cf. Hendricks/Patel/Zeckhauser (1993) p. 94.
[115] Hendricks/Patel/Zeckhauser (1993) p. 102.

redeem their shares in times of worse performance. The last points cause that mutual funds may raise fees to profit from higher AuM as a result of inflows. [116, 117]

Performance persists particularly due to the badly performing funds.[118] These mutual funds have to hold increasing amounts of high liquid assets or cash to fulfill potential redemptions which in addition negatively affect performance.

3.4   Mutual Fund Flows and Determinants

3.4.1   A Brief Overview

The mutual fund flows in the US and United Kingdom (UK) mainly depend on the Morningstar rating and its rating changes. This means that ratings in US and UK indirectly depend on past performance.[119] For this reason it can be assumed that investors implicitly assume past performance as a reliable factor to predict future performance. Otherwise it would be irrational to use past performance as an investing criterion. Unfortunately performance usually is non-persistent over longer horizons.[120] Support for the hypothesis that investors chasing pat performance, is provided by the theoretical paper of Berk and Green arguing "chasing past performance" is rational even when performance is non-persistent and fund managers on average are unable to outperform the market by skill. In detail they claim that funds on average are able to generate a true zero alpha after costs. They assume that managers are endowed with skill which faced decreasing economies of scale. Investors chase the best performing funds as long as all funds would deliver the return of a passive benchmark.[121] This contradicts to the empirical findings of Fama and French who assume that funds are only able to generate a true zero alpha before costs.[122] Consequently the performance after deducting costs is endowed with a negative alpha.

On the European market, fund flows also depended on the mutual fund family, especially if funds are affiliated to a bank. In cases where the mutual fund is not linked to a bank, the findings are quite similar to the US market. But it should be noted that especially the inflows into the top rated funds are smaller.[123]

---

[116] Cf. Del Guercio/Tkac (2008) p. 922, 928; Hendricks/Patel/Zeckhauser (1993) p. 102.
[117] See chapter 4.8 for a more detailed discussion.
[118] Cf. Del Guercio/Tkac (2008) p.919.
[119] Cf. Del Guercio/Tkac (2008) p.909.
[120] Details are discussed in chapter 3.3.
[121] Cf. Berk/Green (2004) p. 1270 - 1272.
[122] Cf. Fama/French (2010) p.1915, 1923.
[123] Cf. Knuutila/Puttonen/Smythe (2007) p. 92 - 94.

It is further noteworthy that fund inflows to performance show a convex shape whereas outflows to performance are u-shaped. This pattern causes that individuals are reluctant to realize loses and, on the same time, are likely to sell winners too early which is called disposition effect.[124] This finding is consistent with the utility function presented in the prospect theory by Kahneman and Tversky.[125]

3.4.2 Mutual Fund Flows and Ratings

The Morningstar rating has a strong influence on fund flows in the US and also on non-bank funds in Europe.[126] The status quo in stars and especially the changes in rating have strong influence on fund flows. In the US markets the normal inflow of five star funds amounts to nearly 85% and four star funds to 40% of total flows, whereas three and two star funds suffer of outflows of nearly 20%. Following that one star funds suffer on outflows of nearly 10% of total normal flows in mutual funds. The remaining flows are distributed on non-rated funds.[127]

Unfortunately there is no study analyzing the "Morningstar effect" for the entire European market. However, we might assume that the Finnish market is quite close to the rest of the European market, in particular regarding the strong focus on the banking sector. The study analyzing the Finish market reported that five star funds collect around 80% and four star funds around 15% of the flows whereas only two star funds suffer from outflows. On the other hand bank funds in Finland show much less dependencies on ratings. In this case average rated (three star) funds receive around 45% and four star funds 20% of the flows. Surprisingly, five star funds receive only 7% of flows, two and one star funds collect 3 % each. The remaining flows are distributed on non-rated funds.[128] In addition bank affiliated funds receive more three star ratings and fewer 2 star ratings and fewer four and five star ratings than non-bank affiliated funds.[129] Summarizing this findings, flows of bank affiliated funds seem to be less sensitive to ratings. This means, even if the fund receives an inferior rating, the fund flow will remain on a quite constant level. This might partly be explained by the strong dominance of banks in Finland. This weaker reaction to ratings respective performance

---

[124] Cf. Jank/Wedow. (2010) p. 2, 11f; Knuutila/Puttonen/Smythe (2007) p. 89.
[125] Cf. Kahneman/Tversky (1979) p. 279.
[126] Cf. Del Guercio/Tkac (2008) p.918; Knuutila/Puttonen/Smythe (2007) p. 89.
[127] Cf. Del Guercio/Tkac (2001) p.37.
[128] Cf. Knuutila/Puttonen/Smythe (2007) p. 94.
[129] Cf. Knuutila/Puttonen/Smythe (2007) p. 91.

is not essentially a drawback for investors since the fund flows in and out of funds are less volatile and trading managers are less affected by liquidity demands.[130]

The study of Del Guercio and Tkac published in 2008 suggest for the US market that especially changes in ratings rather than the rating itself have a strong influence on the fund flows and thus on management incentives.[131] They document that the change in the fund ratings itself has an immediate strong effect on fund flows. They also show that this direct impact is not derived by alternative risk metrics building on assumptions comparable to those used by Morningstar. Interestingly, the asymmetry in the reaction to changes in ratings is even stronger than the asymmetry of normal flows presented above. For example an upgrade from four to five stars cause a 25% increase of flows compared to normal persisting over the seven months following the rating upgrade. An equivalent downgrade on the other hand seems to be a nonevent. Maybe because four star funds are still promoted as high quality, funds are added to retirement plans when receiving five stars but removed when receiving three stars. Downgrades from four to three stars cause outflows 12 times stronger than the normal flows. Whereas a downgrade from three to two stars only leads to abnormal flows of around 25% larger than normal.[132]

3.4.3 Investors and Mutual Fund Flows

Different investor groups show different behavioral patterns when investing in mutual funds. Investors can be differentiated in retail investors and institutional ones. The later can further be distinguished into financial corporations (e.g. banks or mutual funds), insurance companies and pension funds. Retail investors are naive and sophisticated as well, but usually it is assumed that retail investors are rather naive than sophisticated. Institutional investors are indeed sophisticated but especially insurance companies and pension funds are limited in their investment decision due to regulatory constraints.[133] In Germany for example these investors are supervised by the Federal Financial Supervisory Authority (BaFin) which requires the investments to be consistent with the so-called "prudent-man principles".[134] Sophistication in this context means that an

---

[130] Cf. Knuutila/Puttonen/Smythe (2007) p. 89.
[131] Cf. Del Guercio/Tkac (2008) p.928 f..
[132] Cf. Del Guercio/Tkac (2008) p.922, 926 f.
[133] Cf. Jank (2010) p. 2.
[134] Cf. Jank (2010) p. 6.

investor decides based on past performance whereas the decisions of unsophisticated investors are biased by other factors besides performance, like brokerage advice.[135]

Findings for the German market show that financial corporations strongly used to be "chasing past performance", a finding supporting the theoretical framework of Berk and Green. As a result, these investors hold over proportional large assets in the best performing mutual funds. This investor group is followed by pension funds and insurance companies. These firms are also chasing past performance but do this less strongly. This effect is statistically insignificant, which results in an under proportional participation in top performing funds. Pension funds and insurance companies in addition tend to invest in larger, older and less volatile mutual funds which are in line with the prudent-man principles. But these mutual funds are more expensive.[136]

Retail Investors hardly chase past performance. In contrast to institutional investors, their investment flows show a strong and significant tendency of momentum. In particular mutual funds receiving flows of 10% in the current period tend to receive around 2.5% in the following quarter. This finding may be explained by saving plans, advertisings or status quo bias. Such patterns are rather associated with unsophisticated investors.[137] Furthermore, retail investors predominately invest in "marketing-oriented" instead of performance oriented mutual funds, which charge higher fees while performing usually worse. At least theoretically the lower performance might be caused by the more extensive information flow to investors.[138]

Interestingly, only financial corporations punish the worse performing funds by withdrawing their assets of these funds. This evidence is rather weak, following that even the most sophisticated investors show a tendency towards the disposition effect. The remaining investor groups do not react by redeeming their assets when mutual funds show a weak performance,[139] resulting in an even stronger disposition effect.

---

[135] Cf. Jank (2010) p. 5, 6.
[136] Cf. Jank (2010) p. 2, 12.
[137] Cf. Jank (2010) p. 3.
[138] Cf. Davis/Payne/McMahan (2007) p. 323; Golec (2003) 20, 30.
[139] Cf. Jank (2010) p. 13.

4 Determinants and Mutual Fund Performance and (Potential) Problems

4.1 Why Decomposing Fund Performance

As above stated, skill in mutual funds is a scare resource. It is nearly unobservable and has only marginal positive effects on fund performance. In general only unskilled managers have a negative influence on performance. Thus investors should look at other, more persistent and easily observable factors which have or might have influence on performance. In academic literature these factors are widely discussed separately. These factors show some specific characteristics which might have advantages or disadvantages for investors. They are for example:

- Mutual fund fees and expenses
- The fund's affiliation to a bank
- Fund size, asset flows and resulting exit risks
- Board and management structure
- Holdings of the management and board member in the fund or the fund family.
- Education of the management in general but also educational networks[140]

---

[140] See for example: Butler/Gurun (2012); Hao/Yan (2012); Massa/Rehman (2008).

4.2 Mutual Fund Fees and Expenses

4.2.1 A Brief Overview

Mutual fund fees and expenses are directly and easy observable for mutual fund investors. They represent a direct outflow on investors' assets and additionally they are associated with a negative impact on performance.[141] The ongoing fees basically include the remuneration for the management, general administrative costs, trading costs and marketing expenses. Theoretical papers and also some managers argue that high fees are a signal for good managerial skills and thus the price for a good performance.[142] The fees usually differ between different fund types, share classes and even within those groups. In general different funds show different fee structures. These differences are partly explainable due to fund size, the market the fund is invested in or the fund type since some markets are less liquid and / or require more extensive research. Furthermore funds face the adverse price movements when the AuM rise[143], which should be reflected in higher fees. The dispersion in share classes is partly explainable by other fund characteristics like smaller account sizes or more intensive service provided to the customers.[144] Mutual funds set fees strategically in a way that they charge higher fees especially in those funds hold by investors with inelastic demand, (usually retail investors). This pattern results in disproportionally high fees in those mutual funds or share classes which are most common for less sophisticated retail investors. This effect is most pronounced for mutual funds which have front end load fees and are distributed via banks or brokerage firms.[145] The next explanation is quite similar and describes that mutual funds offering relatively low expected returns charge higher fees, since retail investors cannot expect to compete with better performing low expense funds which are hold predominantly by institutional investors and showing a more favorable fee structure.[146] The last argumentation states that weak performing funds increase their marketing expenditures and therefore attract especially unsophisticated retail investors.[147] The conflict of interest in the above mentioned situation is even greater in cases where the fund family itself is traded on exchange, since the mutual fund family

---

[141] Cf. Carhart (1997) p. 58, Tower/Zheng (2008) p. 315.
[142] Cf. Adams/Mansi/Nishikawa (2012) p. 2245 f.; Berk/Green (2004) p. 1277 f.; Smith (2010b) p.52 f..
[143] Cf. Hereil et al. (2010) p. 5; Korkeamaki./Smythe (2004) p. 425.
[144] Cf. Adams/Mansi/Nishikawa (2012) p. 2245 f.; Iannotta/Navone (2012) p. 846 f., 852.; Smith (2010b) p.52 f..
[145] Cf. Christoffersen/Musto (2002) p. 1499; Gil-Bazo/Ruiz-Verdú (2009) p. 2179.
[146] Cf. Gil-Bazo/Ruiz-Verdú (2008) p. 871; Gil-Bazo/Ruiz-Verdú (2009) p. 2179.
[147] Cf. Gil-Bazo/Ruiz-Verdú (2009) p. 2179.

additionally faces pressure from their own shareholders.[148] Fees and expenses are important for investors when buying mutual funds, since they represent a direct reduction on investors' assets. It should be noted that they are persistent which is represented by a r-square of 0.77 when regressing these years' expenses and last years' expenses.[149] This persistence causes that investors are able to reliable calculate the asset outflow induced by fees for the next periods.

4.2.2 Multiple Share Classes and Fees

Multiple share class funds for retail investors in the USA have been introduced in the early 1990s. This has led funds and fund families offering fund share classes specialized on different investor's clienteles and purposes, by providing diverse alternative fee and load structures. In 2002, 50% of mutual funds in the US offered at least two different share classes. At the same time the number of no-load funds has increased in a similar way.[150] During that process the spread in expense ratios between load and no-load funds has significantly increased and remains high. Usually load funds are more prevalent to retail investors and no-load funds are more common for institutional investors.[151]

Multiple share class funds are of interest for funds because only the investing clients and the flow pattern change, whereas the management and the fund objectives remain the same. The flows increase and become more volatile which erodes fund performance. This is one essential drawback for fund investors, especially long term retail investors, the decline in performance may become stronger when fund suffer from net outflows. The level of this impact is related to the sensitivity of investors to performance.[152, 153]

Before multiple share class funds were introduced, load funds on average charged lower annual expense ratios than no-load funds. This approach is in line with the intuition and statement of mutual fund managers that funds with (higher) front loads should have lower ongoing expenses and thus investors should be able to capture these expenses over long investment horizons. Unfortunately, after the introduction of multiple share class funds, the expense ratio of load funds is about on average 50 basis points higher

---

[148] Cf. Adams/Mansi/Nishikawa (2012) p. 2245.
[149] Cf. Bechmann/Rangvid (2007) p. 664, 684.
[150] Cf. Nanda/Wang/Zheng (2009) p. 329.
[151] Cf. Adams/Mansi/Nishikawa (2012) p. 2245; Houge /Wellman (2006) p. 27; Nanda/Wang/Zheng (2009) p. 329 f.
[152] Cf. Nanda/Wang/Zheng (2009) p. 331, 343.
[153] For a further discussion see chapter 3.4.

24

than the expense ratios of their no-load counterparts instead. In this context it seems kind cynical that, mutual fund executives still claim that investors in load funds can capture their higher initial costs by lower expense ratios in the long run.[154]

Especially unsophisticated retail investors suffer from such cost structures, which are used by mutual funds to provide their more sophisticated investors even better conditions.[155] This pattern is possible since mutual funds do not document how the costs are spread on different share classes.[156] In addition, the smaller the wealth an investor wants to invest the larger is the share of his search costs. Thus investors face a trade-off between search costs and a potentially better investment alternative. Consequently investors are only willing to redeem the "old" mutual fund and purchase a "new" one if the potential gain of the alternative fund exceeds the search costs. This pattern is most present in funds invested in small markets with only a few competitors. Consequently mutual funds with many competitors are much likely to provide funds with a fair fee structure simply due to market force.[157] Funds on the other hand react on their competitors and focus on advertising and brand name development to lower their investors' search costs. This increase in marketing expenditures is paid by relatively higher fees which are deducted from the return received by investors.[158] In addition fund families commonly offer their investors to switch between different mutual funds within the family without or at least without further costs.[159] Nevertheless investors face the risk of being unable to predict future performance of any fund, which makes the decision even more difficult.

Additional reasons why such dispersions in fees are possible become apparent when observing the behavior of mutual fund investors. In a competitive market, one would assume that index mutual funds with inappropriate high costs would leave the market, since their pre-expense returns are virtually the same and consequently the expenses should be the "only" investment criterion.[160] In an experimental environment with "real" incentives, investors should choose a mutual index fund mirroring the S&P 500. Nearly every "investor" fails to choose low cost mutual index funds. In contrast investors look above all on past performance since the fund was initiated, even when

---

[154] Cf. Houge /Wellman (2006) p. 26, 32.
[155] Cf. Houge /Wellman (2006) p. 23.
[156] Cf. Adams/Mansi/Nishikawa (2012) p. 2246.
[157] Cf. Adams/Mansi/Nishikawa (2012) p. 2246; Jank/Wedow. (2010) p. 2.
[158] Cf. Davis/Payne/McMahan (2007) p. 323; Golec (2003) 20; Sirri,/Tufano (1998) p.1590.
[159] Cf. Jank/Wedow. (2010) p. 2.
[160] Cf. Choi/Laibson/Madrian (2010) p. 1406 f.; Houge /Wellman (2006) p. 26, 32.

funds have different inception dates and the provided brochures have different print dates. In reality some investors would have paid roughly 2% per year more than they needed to, while receiving virtually the same pre-expense return. The results are especially remarkable, as all participants on this experiment show above average literacy, some also have further skills in business administration and some have at least a few years' experience in managing their own portfolio.[161, 162]

Overall retail investors might still profit when investing in retail funds with an institutional twin (multiple share class funds), even when they might pay "inadequately" high fees. This effect might largely be induced by the unfavorable characteristics of load funds. [163] The introduction of an institutional twin in general causes a decrease in expense ratios, as well as an increase in the performance.[164] This performance difference amounts to 1.5% annually compared to funds without an institutional twin. This can be explained by the fact that institutional investors are able and willing to monitor the funds better than retail investors.[165] Beyond that, institutional investors are more likely to vote with their feet by redeeming their shares.

This described mechanism results in a positive performance flow relation and thus gives incentives for mutual fund managers to perform well.[166] Furthermore, institutional holdings have a positive influence on the "pay-for-performance sensitivities".[167] This leads to the fact that funds with institutional holdings are up to 20% less likely involved in scandals and abusive actions than "pure" retail funds. These mutual funds show lower or even negative performance flow sensitivity, which is a clear indication for the disposition effect and thus unsophisticated investors.[168]

4.2.3 Corporate Elements and Fees

High fees are associated with some unfavorable corporate structures for investors. These are for example the board structure and an inadequate high level of the managerial fees (remuneration). High, or more precisely inadequately high fees, suggest that the board is

---

[161] Cf. Choi/Laibson/Madrian (2010) p. 1406 f..

[162] This finding might be in line with the findings of Kahnemann and Tversky (1979) that individuals are underestimate small probabilities and amounts (fees charged in comparison to the performance).

[163] Cf. Houge/Wellman (2006) p. 26.

[164] Cf. Evans/Fahlenbrach (2012) p. 3530 f..

[165] Beyond that insurance companies and pension funds are forced by the BaFin to act with the prudent-man principles and thus these should be less tolerant in regard of bad performance, see Cf. Jank (2010) p. 6 and chapter 3.4.3.

[166] Cf. Evans/Fahlenbrach (2012) p. 3530 f..

[167] Cf. Matsumura/Shin (2005) p. 107.

[168] Cf. Qian, M. (2011) p. 46.

unable to protect the shareholders' interests.[169] In the United States of America (USA) the Investment Company Act allows litigations against excessive fees liabilities. Regarding this liability it is interesting that only the theory of an excessive fee justifies a lawsuit, initiated by the Securities and Exchange Commission (SEC) or every investor. The possibility to be sued due to excessive fees causes that funds improve their fee and expense structure as well as their governance structure, which is usually costly. Fund families sued tend to increase their fees. However, the most expensive funds, which are likely to be retail funds, become cheaper. Especially the biggest mutual fund families are more likely to be sued, even if their fees and expenses are "less" excessive compared to smaller families.[170] The litigation may represent some a kind of external disciplinary mechanism which decreases the incentives of mutual funds to charge inadequately high fees to their investors. Excessive fee litigations need not essentially to be disclosed. That's why these litigations are usually hardly noticed by the public and thereafter have only minor impact on the fund family's reputation.[171]

4.3   Board and Management Linked Parameters

4.3.1   A Brief Overview

The fund board and the management are often seen as the source of a mutual fund's success or fail. Astonishingly these sources are likely to be underestimated or even ignored by investors, at least in the past. The market timing scandals in the US can be seen as a wakeup call because they causes regulatory changes. In this context, Morningstar introduces its Stewardship rating, which only rates corporate factors.[172, 173] A recent study suggests that investors take into account these corporate factors by looking at the Morningstar stewardship rating.[174] The corporate factors could be differentiated in the following way:

- The overall governance structure of the fund
  - Linkages between the board and the management (investment advisors)
  - Proportion of independent board members
  - Background of board members and their independence
- The Managers itself and directly linked points

---

[169] Gil-Bazo/Ruiz-Verdú (2009) p. 2168; Adams/Mansi/Nishikawa (2012) p. 2246.
[170] Curtis, Q./Morley, J. (2012) p. 3.
[171] Curtis, Q./Morley, J. (2012) p. 5.
[172] Cf. Gottesman/Morey (2012) p. 69; Morningstar Inc. (2010b) p.1, 2.
[173] The Morningstar Stewardship rating is discussed in detail in chapter 4.6.2.
[174] Cf. Wellman/Zhou (2008) p.1.

- Remuneration and Incentives
- Educational background of managers

4.3.2   Linkages between the Fund Board and the Management

Theoretically at least 75% of US mutual fund board members should be independent and the board members should deal at arms-length with the advisors and managers of the fund, respectively. When looking at SEC requirements, independency is defined as whether a board member or a member of her firm is employed at the fund advisor.[175] This definition is questionable when looking at the way a mutual fund is initiated and board members are selected. When mutual funds are initiated the advisory firm is the only shareholder and she consequently appoints all board members. In the ongoing business the advisor's shares become relatively unimportant. Nevertheless, future changes of the board's composition are not mandatory and usually do not take place.

SEC requires annually re-evaluations of the fund's advisory contracts. A further evidence: Changes of the advisory firm for the three medium performance quintile funds are associated with an increased subsequent mutual fund performance. These evidences raise the serious question whether the board really acts in the best interests of the shareholders and whether the board is rather likely to support the advisor than the fund investors. Changing fund advisors for weak performing funds has no impact on subsequent performance, but a negative impact on top performing funds. But this should not be an argument for the board to be reluctant for changing the advisor, since (retail) investors do not "vote with their feet" by redeeming their shares[176] and do not harm the funds' assets.

From a rather theoretical point of view this connection might be advantageous for shareholders, as board members and managers (advisors) share information. With increased assets under management, the board members usually hire additional investment advisors (sub advisors).[177]

The hiring process of sub advisors is mainly determined by the connectivity between the board and the sub advisor which is not essentially a drawback for investors. A reason for this pattern might be that a close connectivity reduces search costs and monitoring the same is also easier comparable to an unknown manager. These search costs are especially high in those funds associated with high(er) managerial skill and lower in

---

[175] Cf. Kuhnen (2009) p. 2188.
[176] Cf. Kuhnen (2005) p. 6 - 8; Kuhnen (2009) p. 2186.
[177] Cf. Kuhnen (2009) p. 2186.

28

funds which require less managerial skill or those funds where skill is more easily identifiable, respectively, like index funds. Given the fact that changes of the advisory firm, are more likely in larger fund families and for example in index funds. The same author states in a different paper that costs and specialization, which can be seen as kind of skill, seem nearly unimportant when hiring sub-advisors.[178]

4.3.3 The Structure of Fund Management

The mutual fund portfolios are either managed by a single manager or multiple managers. This distinction refers to the final decision making. These managers are usually belonging to (different) investment advisors. Multiple manager funds could be further distinguished into team and co-managed funds. In team managed funds the decision process is carried out by the team as a whole, whereas in co-managed funds every manager manages a specific segment. Virtually every mutual fund has some or at least one investment advisor, which might be external or internal to mutual fund families. These advisors are usually responsible for the day to day business of the fund, which makes the decision process much more complicated than simply assuming multiple or single manager funds.[179]

In general it could be stated that the number of multiple manager mutual funds has increased in recent years.[180] Their share amounted 30% or nearly 60% in 2004 depending on the definition used and the treatment of those mutual funds which do not publish the names of their managers.[181] The percentage of mutual funds which do not disclose the names of their managers' amounts nearly 20% in 2004, although these funds are likely to be team managed.[182] Multiple manager funds are most likely managed by a management team and at least one investment advisor. Their percentage amounts around 70% in the year 2004.[183]

Especially the effect of team management in (organizations) mutual funds in the regard of risk assumption and performance is remaining unclear. In general teams are associated with slower but maybe wiser decision making processes which also help to

---

[178] Cf. Kuhnen (2005) p. 7f.; Kuhnen (2009) p. 2187 f..
[179] Cf. Karagiannidis (2010) p. 198 - 200.
[180] Cf. Karagiannidis (2010) p. 198.
[181] Cf. Bär/Kempf/Ruenzi (2011) p. 367; Karagiannidis (2010) p. 200 f.; Massa/Reuter/Zitzewitz (2010) p. 401.
[182] Cf. Massa/Reuter/Zitzewitz (2010) p. 401.
[183] Cf. Karagiannidis (2010) p. 200.

avoid serious errors occurring due to individual mistakes.[184] Theoretical and experimental studies suggest that management teams tend to be more risky. This effect is induced by a dominant manager and is called the **group shift hypothesis**. In this hypothesis groups tend towards the extreme and are slower in their decision making process, at least when looking at "important" decisions.[185] The first empirical study regarding the behavior of teams shows the reverse results. This finding builds on the **diversification of opinions theory** and states that different team members control each other, which result in less risky and less extreme outcomes. Thus team decisions are more likely to show a lower risk proportion than decisions made by individuals.[186] Team managed mutual funds show more diversified and less industry concentrated portfolios than mutual funds managed by a single manager. This pattern increases with the number of team members. Thus those funds usually show less extreme returns than single manager funds, which results in a more stable performance.[187]

When looking solely on the performance, there is no difference observable between single and team managed mutual funds, as long as they have only one investment advisor. Team managed funds with two or more advisors perform worse than team managed mutual funds with only one advisor in bear markets and in growth funds.[188] This finding might be explainable due to the fact that team managed funds, especially in cases of turmoil, are disposition prone compared to single managed ones. Resulting in the fact that those funds predominantly sell winners and hold loses too long.[189] The previous argumentation regarding the benefits and drawbacks of team management should not apply for co-managed funds, since the decision process is similar to single-managed funds.

As before mentioned, some mutual funds do not disclose the names of their management. Mutual funds which disclose and maybe promote the names of their top managers receive higher investor inflows and single manager might be more motivated to perform well, since her name is linked to the performance. On the other hand the manager's bargaining power increases which might reduce the firm's rent and later on the managers are quite likely to increase the risk proportion.[190, 191]

---

[184] Cf. Bär/Kempf/Ruenzi (2011) p.361; Massa/Reuter/Zitzewitz (2010) p. 401; Sah/Stiglitz (1988) p. 451 f..
[185] Cf. Bär/Kempf/Ruenzi (2011) p.359 f.; Kerr (1992) p.64, 92.
[186] Cf. Bär/Kempf/Ruenzi (2011) p.359 f.; Sah/Stiglitz (1988) p. 469 f..
[187] Cf. Bär/Kempf/Ruenzi (2011) p.361.
[188] Cf. Karagiannidis (2010) p. 199.
[189] Cf. Cici (2012) p. 796.
[190] Cf. Massa/Reuter/Zitzewitz (2010) p. 401 f..

Mutual fund managers' tenure amounts four years on average, thus changes in the top management of mutual funds are quite common.[192] A change in the top management of mutual funds usually results in change of the performance. These mutual funds, regardless whether they have under or over-performed before the management left the fund, voluntarily or was replaced, tend to be averagely performing in the period thereafter.[193] A study analyzing the impact on each performance quintile summarizes that the three medium quintiles performing mutual funds tend to perform better whereas the best performance quantile performed worse.[194] Hence mutual funds are strongly and directly affected in cases when shareholders redeem their shares. The replacement of the fund management could therefore be a quite important government mechanism to stop investors redeeming their shares and thus harming the mutual fund.[195, 196]

In the time before the management of bad performing funds was replaced, these mutual funds show significant higher outflows, induced by bad performance. In addition these funds increase their portfolio risk and also their portfolio turnover. This is associated with the notion that managers want to catch with the top performing funds and also tend to window-dress their portfolio. Window-dressing in this case means that these managers start to imitate the holdings of top performing funds and also invest in the former momentum stocks. Additionally, this finding is consistent with the hypothesis that managers which have performed worse tend to increase the risk of their portfolios. Consequently in the post replacement period the portfolio turnover and the portfolio risk also decline.[197]

These market reactions might be a good reason for the mutual fund board to implement management teams or do not publish the names of the managers in general. When only one manager of a team is replaced, it is easy arguable that this replacement has virtually no or only minor impacts on performance. This might result in a more stable performance pattern and a smaller investor flow reaction.

[191] For a more detailed discussion see: Massa/Reuter/Zitzewitz (2010).
[192] Cf. Chevalier/Ellison (1999a) p.880; Fu, R./Wedge, L. (2011) p. 2411.
[193] Cf. Khorana. (2001) p. 372; Massa/Reuter/Zitzewitz (2010) p. 401.
[194] Cf. Kuhnen (2005) p. 6.
[195] Cf. Khorana (2001) p. 376.
[196] See also: Denis/Denis (1995) They documented for forced top management (CEO) resignation during the years 1988 to 1995 that the operative performance has significantly improved after these managers were replaced.
[197] Cf. Khorana (2001) p. 373, 385.

4.3.4 Mutual Fund Manager's Characteristics

Since mutual fund manager are one of the elementary sources of mutual fund performance, it is worth to look at them. Studies suggest that there are indeed some manager characteristics' which are linked to superior performance. Problems by identifying these patterns in mutual funds originate from the fact that there are rarely single managed mutual funds. Fortunately, other studies focusing on hedge funds deliver quite similar results. All these studies indicate that the average SAT score (Scholastic Assessment Test) of the managers undergraduate school is positively correlated to the fund performance.[198] But it is also possible that these differences are due to the fact that managers with different "skills" work for different funds [199]

Managers with an MBA outperform those without an MBA by more than 0.5% annually due to more systematic risk evaluation. This might be due to inherent abilities or benefits from their higher education.

Managers who are 12 years younger than the average manager outperform those by one percent point per year. This pattern is induced also by lower fees and survivorship bias and do not indicated superior skill, thus when looking at the manager's age, only a small fraction in performance difference remains, which is "really" linked to the managers' age.[200] These differences might be induced by harder work, since younger managers are more likely to be terminated for bad performance. Additionally, those managers have their careers in front of them and their careers might be ruined by a bad track record.[201] Another explanation to this finding is that older managers are less likely to be terminated, because they are likely to stay longer within the same mutual fund (family) and thus might have built some empire. In this case independent directors might solve the problem.[202] But older managers are likely to be better connected with board members which in favor are reluctant to terminate those managers.[203] The termination risk is also lower for internal managers. This lower termination risks result in a more risky behavior of such internal managers.[204]

---

[198] Cf. Chevalier/Ellison (1999a) p.875; Li/Zhang/Zhao (2011) p. 59.
[199] Cf. Chevalier/Ellison (1999a) p.877.
[200] Cf. Chevalier/Ellison (1999a) p. 876 f..
[201] Cf. Chevalier/Ellison (1999a) p. 877; Chevalier/Ellison (1999b) p. 389.
[202] Cf. Ding/Wermers (2012) p. 4 f..
[203] Cf. Kuhnen (2009) p. 2185 f..
[204] Cf. Elton/Gruber/Blake (2003) p. 784.

Younger managers in addition tend to be involved in herding and they tend to invest in "popular" sectors, furthermore they show relative low exposure to unsystematic risk.[205] The lower exposure to unsystematic risk taking is consistent with less skill but also with less valuable or smaller networks.

An alternative explanation might be that managers with MBAs and those visiting undergraduate schools with higher reputation (higher average SAT score) have better networks. These networks are valuable since fund managers investing predominantly in those funds whose managers and board members are in the same educational network. The return difference in portfolios of connected and unconnected holdings amounted 7.8% annually. In addition the virtually same portfolio of connected stocks hold by connected and unconnected managers shows a return difference of about 6.8 % annually.[206] Almost the entire difference in performance is allocated around corporate news releases, which strongly suggest that fund managers are endowed with some private information. This contradicts the hypothesis that the information flow is due to "fewer calls". This also refutes the assumption that mutual fund managers are more aware of the action of the firm managers since they have similar educational backgrounds. The existence of such networks becomes apparent when observing the changes in holdings following a management turnover. Here especially those stocks are sold where the former managers were connected to and those purchased to which the incoming manager is connected to.[207]

The existence of such networks and especially the existence of a direct information flow to fund managers are supported by two different findings. First due to the reason that the superior performance around the earnings announcements has declined after the year 2000. In that year the SEC required a fair disclosure of news to all shareholders and prohibited selective corporate information disclosure.[208] Second due to the fact that mutual fund managers belonging to the same educational network like the managers of those firms they are invested in tend to vote in the favor of these managers, especially by shareholder proposals regarding excess compensation. This effect becomes stronger with when voting is repeated.[209]

---

[205] Cf. Chevalier/Ellison (1999b) p. 389.
[206] Cf. Cohen/Frazzini/Malloy (2008) p. 951 - 954.
[207] Cf. Butler/Gurun (2012) p. 2533 - 2535; Cohen/Frazzini/Malloy (2008) p. 951 - 954.
[208] Cf. Baker et al. (2010) p. 1113.
[209] Cf. Butler/Gurun (2012) p. 2533.

4.4   Exits in Mutual Funds

Exits in mutual funds are quite common and have or may have serious consequences for investors, since investors are likely to lose their investment objective. On the other hand, given that usually weakly performing funds are more likely to be affected by exits, investors in the exited fund might even profit, especially in case of merger. In detail, in the time span starting 1992 and ending 2003, one out of five mutual funds were exited. Between 1962 and 1999 mergers affected one out of six mutual funds.[210] The decision of exits usually originates in the fund family and not in the mutual funds itself, since the fund operates in a broader family. In general exits occur in three different forms:

- **Liquidation** describes a situation where investors usually have the opportunity to transfer their assets to another mutual fund within the same family, before "their" mutual fund is liquidated and their originally investment objective is lost.

- **Within-family** and **across-family merger** describe situations where a fund is merged into another fund within the same mutual fund family or in another fund family, respectively. Investors usually have the same options than described above.[211] Mergers may be attractive for funds due to some economies of scale as long as the resulting fund is not "too" large and thus faces adverse price movements.[212]

The risk of merger increases in bear and bull markets. Examples are the turmoil around the oil crisis in 1970s or the new economy bubble at the end 1990s.[213] The same should also apply for liquidations. More precisely, exit decisions in funds affect funds basically in three different situations:

- **Shrinking** funds suffer from significant cash outflows.
- **Stagnant** funds still grow but their growth rate is below the average growth rate.
- **Redundant** funds may still perform well and show above average growth rates, but these funds have a sister fund within the same financial conglomerate and thus face the risk of mergers, otherwise there would be risks of cannibalization.[214]

I assume that shrinking funds usually perform worse and are first time rated an inferior Morningstar rating when they are at least three years old. Hence, investors should be

---

[210] Cf. Ding (2006) p. 1; Zhao (2005) p. 1372 - 1374.
[211] Zhao, X. (2005) p. 1365 f..
[212] Cf. Ding, (2006) p. 10, 13.
[213] Cf. Ding, (2006) p. 14.
[214] Cf. Ding, (2006) p. 8.

able to identify these shrinking funds quite easily. Redundant and stagnant funds are not or hardly observable for investors, since investors need detailed information about fund holdings and asset flows of at least one fund. Consequently investors might have only small chances to actively avoid such funds.

The following statements are most prevalent to shrinking and partly to stagnant funds. Exit decisions are more likely for smaller, younger and weak performing funds and funds charging higher fees[215]. Only the smallest funds with low inflows are likely to become subject of liquidation. The reasons are their ongoing expenses which are linked to the AuM, hence they are hardly in the position to cover the costs. Weak performance is only important in cases of within-family mergers.[216] In addition fund families tend to terminate funds with only a few share classes. Mutual funds offering an unique portfolio are much more likely to liquidated or sold to another family. Within-family merger are more likely to occur in bigger fund families. Funds with more share classes and with back-end fees are more likely to be merged, since otherwise the family would lose some future revenues. In general mergers are much more likely between funds with similar investment strategies, because this lowers the implementation costs. Thus investors in the acquired fund may even profit, since the acquiring mutual fund usually performs better than the acquired fund and have a similar investment objective.[217]

Generally, exits in mutual funds may discipline underperformers and might be positive for the entire mutual fund market, since badly performing funds should vanish. Unfortunately this mechanism does not capture "all" weak performing funds.[218] The exit decision is linked to board characteristics because the board usually initiates the merger. Especially across-family mergers are more likely in rather independent boards since these boards are less tolerant against bad performance. This pattern even persists in the range of above 75% board independency, as required by the SEC. On the other hand higher paid boards are less likely to initiate across-family mergers. This can be explained by the fact that the board members would lose their board seats and thus compensation.[219] This represents a conflict of interest and leads to further doubts

---

[215] Note that the causality at this point is not entirely clear, since the chapter above stated, performance and fees are negatively correlated.
[216] Cf. Brown/Goetzmann (1995) p. 684, 686; Ding, (2006) p. 8; Khorana/Tufano/Wedge (2007a) p. 573; Zhao (2005) p.1367.
[217] Cf. Zhao (2005) p. 1367.
[218] Cf. Brown/Goetzmann (1995) p. 680.
[219] Cf. Khorana/Tufano/Wedge (2007a) p. 571 f.

whether the board members really "serve as "independent watchdogs," guarding investor interests"[220] as required by the SEC.

In this context another problem occurs because the performance in the acquiring fund is usually negatively affected since decreasing economies of scale in managerial talents and investors in those funds are not aware of such actions. Across-family mergers are of interest for the acquiring fund since the acquiring of another mutual fund represents a relative easy way to increase the fee income, even if the expected performance declines and investors are hurt. In addition those unfavorable across-family deals are more likely in publicly hold funds and funds with a rather weak board. This kind of fund families faces stronger pressure to perform well due to the fact that they face analysts' pressure.[221]

4.5   Bank Affiliation

4.5.1   A Brief Overview

Mutual funds affiliated to a bank show a stronger prevalence to the conflict of interest, since the fund management is a kind of double agent.[222] On the one hand they have fiduciary duties towards the investors in the fund[223]; but in the end they are paid by the bank which operates other businesses as well. The importance of bank affiliation might become apparent when looking at the USA where about 40% of mutual funds are affiliated to a bank. These funds may have more and better research resources, lower transaction costs and distribution externalities, and in some cases superior information about the clients of the affiliated bank. This information results from initial public offerings business (IPO), seasoned equity offerings (SEO) business as well as from the bank's credit business. Thus at least some of this information is not available for "ordinary" market participants and represents consequently private information. The usage of their information would be insider trading and violates the law.[224]

---

[220] SEC (1999) p. 2.
[221] Cf. Berk/Green (2004) p. 1271; Ferris/Yan (2009) p. 619 f..
[222] Cf. Davis/Payne/McMahan (2007) p. 323.
[223] Cf Mehran/Stulz (2007) p. 268.
[224] Cf. Hao/Yan (2012) p. 537 f.; Massa/Rehman (2008) p. 288 f..

4.5.2   Affiliation to Investment Banks

Regarding funds or fund families affiliated to an investment bank, these funds or fund families are assumed to show larger participation rates in those SEO and IPO client's stocks which show higher likelihoods of high future abnormal returns compared to the market and vice versa.[225] These characteristics should result in superior performance in investment bank affiliated mutual funds compared to non-bank affiliated funds.

The empirical finding shows that mutual funds affiliated to an investment bank indeed have over proportionately high holdings in the stocks of IPOs and the SEOs of their affiliated investment bank client's. Unfortunately mutual funds tend to hold those SEO and IPO stocks which perform worse and rather than those stocks more likely to perform well. Consequently these mutual funds perform significantly worse than comparable non-investment bank affiliated funds and investors in those funds are adversely affected by the fund's affiliation to an investment bank. The underperformance amounts approximately 1% up to 1.7% per year. Even when adding back the fees, there is still a significant underperformance of roughly 0.7% to 1.4% per year. One third up to one half of this difference is explainable due to the holdings in the SEO and IPO stocks of the affiliated investment bank.[226] A slightly older study supports this effect but also finds evidence for a reverse effect stating that fund investors may also profit from the affiliation to an investment bank, which is called the "nepotism hypothesis".[227] The most recent study analyzing the years 1990 to 2008 finds also evidence that investors in mutual funds affiliated to investments banks suffer in most of the years.[228] The alpha amounted -0.46% per year for bank affiliated funds compared to funds not affiliated to investment banks. Only in five out of 19 years investors profit from information advantages of the affiliated investment bank. In the remaining 14 years the costs overweighed the benefits of the affiliation to an investment bank.[229]

The reasons for these findings are apparent when looking closer at the investment bank and the fund family. These financial institutions generate the vast majority (up to 65%) of their revenues in the investment banking business and below 10% in their mutual fund business. These dealings are consistent with the "dumping ground" hypothesis, which describes that investment banks allocate their "cold" IPOs to affiliated mutual

---

[225] Cf. Hao/Yan (2012) p.563.

[226] Cf. Hao/Yan (2012) p. 539.

[227] Cf. Ritter./Zhang (2007) p.337, 339.

[228] The results for hedge funds, institutional funds and mutual are quite similar, even when mutual funds carry most of the costs. See Berzins/Liu/Trzcinka (2013) p. 2 - 5.

[229] Cf. Berzins/Liu/Trzcinka (2013) p. 2 - 5, 44.

funds in order to boost IPO performance and win future underwriting business. Mutual fund managers support these SEOs and IPOs even though these investments harm fund performance and mutual fund investors. Fund managers participate on those practices since their compensation schemes are not solely linked to the mutual fund attributes and thus on investors' welfare.[230, 231]

The results remain fairly unchanged when looking only at the top ten investment banks. This supports the assumption that this problem is widespread in the mutual fund industry. In addition, it is unlikely that these results are driven by lower skilled managers in investment bank affiliated mutual funds. Reasonably assuming that the top banks like Morgan Stanley or Goldman Sachs are indeed be able to attract top skilled mutual fund managers, consequently these managers should be able to generate at least average performance.[232]

4.5.3 Credit Bank Affiliation and General Conflicts with Bank Affiliation

Credit bank affiliated mutual funds show increased (decreased) participation rates in those firms which are likely to perform well (worse) in cases where the affiliated credit bank has business contacts.[233] As a result these mutual funds show indeed a better performance than their non-credit bank affiliated counterparts. This effect seems to be driven by superior information within the financial conglomerates and is most prevalent for younger, smaller and worst performing funds.[234] For this reason it can be assumed that these companies might use the described actions to stay on the market, respective to receive some market shares. Another potential drawback has been uncovered in Spain, where bank affiliated funds tend to support the stock of their parent's bank when they suffer price drops. Mutual fund managers act, at least in the short run, in the interest of the bank and its shareholders and not in the interest of the investors of the mutual fund, who usually suffer from such actions. In the long run these tradings might have also consequences for the bank shareholders, since a worse performing fund might suffer from outflows which affect also the parent bank.[235] I assume that these support purchases are not limited to the Spanish market and may be of interest for the entire mutual fund market.

---

[230] Cf. Hao/Yan (2012) p. 538, 549; Farnsworth/Taylor (2006) p. 305; Ritter./Zhang (2007) p.339.
[231] For further detail on the remuneration see chapter 4.8.2.
[232] Cf. Hao/Yan (2012) p. 540, 557.
[233] Cf. Massa/Rehman (2008) p.291.
[234] Cf. Massa/Rehman (2008) p.288 ff..
[235] Cf. Golez/Marin (2012) p. 1 - 3.

Mutual funds involved in such conflict of interest face at least theoretically the risk that these actions are not in line with the law, which may result in serious law suits, fines and damage of reputation. Investors might also be harmed since these funds suffer increased outflows which deteriorate performance even though the management is substantially good.

In Europe the conflict of interest might be even more prevalent due to the fact that, in contrast to the US market, mutual funds are manly distributed via their affiliated bank. Such affiliated banks tend to distribute their own funds, even if other funds have performed better in the past.[236] This finding is not necessarily worse for investors because the inflows and outflows in these funds are less volatile and fund managers might be able to anticipate future investor flows.[237] As a result the funds might perform more constantly and better in the long run than funds facing more unforeseeable investor flows. In addition, a more persistent performance lowers the risk for investors of buying and selling on discount or premium.

4.6 Corporate Elements and Performance

4.6.1 A Brief Overview

The corporate structure and governance in mutual funds has received increasing attention in recent years. Some firms with certain corporate structures are less likely to be involved in such abusive actions, as the aftermath of the market timing and late trading scandals have shown. Compared to the fund performance, these elements are usually not easily observable. But in contrast to fund performance these elements are rather persistent. Some of these elements are able to predict performance, whereas others show rather co-movements with the fund performance. Incorporating those elements when analyzing mutual funds might be quite valuable for investors. Some corporate elements are already discussed above.

---

[236] Cf. Knuutila/Puttonen/Smythe (2007) p. 92
[237] For a further discussion see 3.4.2.

4.6.2 Morningstar Stewardship Rating

In this section I will introduce the Morningstar stewardship rating for mutual funds, since it is most the developed standard and also widely available for investors. Furthermore, this rating is already discussed by academics.[238] Hence it is possible to assess the usefulness and value of the rating and its single elements.

The purpose of the Morningstar stewardship rating is to provide investors some help to identify those mutual funds which show favorable and unfavorable corporate characteristics. Similar to the star rating, Morningstar points out that this rating is rather a guideline than a direct recommendation to buy or to sell a certain mutual fund. The final score of the Stewardship rating builds on the five elements below:

- **Corporate Culture** amounts to 40% of the total score and incorporates especially the fiduciary duties. Aspects analyzed are the way the fund discloses information and the sustainability of the investment process.

- **Board Quality** accounts for 20% of the score and describes the alignment of the board with the investors. In more detail it analyzes whether the fund acts in the investors' "best interest". Rather quantitative aspects are the independence of the board and the holdings of independent board members in the funds they oversee. In contrast, employees of the fund, the fund family or any service providers, even former ones, are not seen as independent. At least 75% of board members should be independent, which is in line with the requirements of the SEC. At least 75% of the independent board members should hold assets at least as big as their annual compensation.

- **Manager Incentives** amounts to 20% and contains the remuneration structure and the managerial holdings. Here a compensation structure which supports the long-term development is considered as positive. Consequently, a compensation structure which focuses on the short run and supports asset growth is seen as negative.

- The **Fees** score amounts to 20% and reflects in which quintile the funds ongoing expenses are located, funds in the highest quantile receive the highest score whereas funds in the lowest one receive no score.

---

[238] See for example: Chen/Huang (2011); Chou/Ng./Wang (2011); Gottesman/Morey (2012); Wellman/ Zhou (2008).

- The **Regulatory History** amounts -20% and is only taken into account, when if the fund have faced "regulatory issues" in recent years, and only "serious breaches" result in a reduction of the total score of 20%.[239]

4.6.3 The Influence of Fund Governance on Mutual Fund Holdings

The academic literature gives different pictures when talking about the importance of corporate governance.[240] Sometimes it is argued that mutual funds "only" care about the expected return and a good governance of the stocks in their portfolio is rather a side effect. Thus mutual funds are more likely to vote with their feet in cases when they detect bad governance or abusive actions which might have consequences on the stock price.[241] Other studies suggest that institutional investors have indeed recognized the importance of a good governance structure of the firm whose stock they buy and increase their holdings in case of good governance. This behavior is consistent with the fiduciary duties of institutional investors and also with minimization of monitoring costs.[242] This is the reason why better governed firms in general are less likely to be involved in abusive actions or white collar crime. At this point investors should be careful since some aspects might have negative consequences as well. [243]

Going further, a good corporate culture is also able to prevent white collar crimes and identifies also "formal cross-company communication" and performance-related pay for board members. Here especially an option-based payment structure is most effective.[244] This is interesting from different perspectives.

First, an option-based payment for board members indirectly represents a holding in the firm, which has, as above mentioned, a positive effect on performance due to a better alignment with the shareholders.

Second, a performance-related pay might reduce the incentives of board members to participate in many different boards ("busy" board members) at the same time. This might be important considering the fact that independent board members having seats in three or more different boards show a higher tolerance in regard of weak performing managers. Board with many busy board members show similar patterns like those boards dominated by non-independent directors. Consequently those companies are

---

[239] Cf. Morningstar Inc. (2010b) p. 2.
[240] See for example: Chung/Zhang (2011); Matsumura/Shin (2005); Schnatterly (2003).
[241] Cf. Matsumura/Shin (2005) p.107 f..
[242] Cf. Chung/Zhang (2011) p. 247, 264.
[243] Cf. Schnatterly (2003) p. 587.
[244] Cf. Schnatterly (2003) p. 587, 606.

associated with weak governance. [245] In the case of mutual funds, this might be directly reflected in an inferior performance.

More interesting is indeed the finding that mutual fund's stewardship rating itself is positively correlated to the corporate quality of the stocks in the mutual fund portfolio. In more detail those mutual funds have relatively more holdings of "good" governed stocks than of "bad" governed stocks in their portfolio. [246] In addition those funds with a superior stewardship rating are more committed in monitoring those firms. They vote in the interest of their mutual fund investors especially in corporate governance related issues. In contrast to that, rather weak governed mutual funds (inferior stewardship rating) tend to vote in the favor of the management the fund is invested in. [247, 248]

The more intensive participation of good governed funds in their portfolio is somewhat surprising, since active monitoring and participation in proxy votes is associated with higher costs. As a consequence it is commonly assumed that mutual funds do not participate in such actions and rather vote with their feet and sell their shares when they discover corporate wrongdoing. Interestingly, those funds, despite of their higher costs, do not underperform their peers. Results furthermore suggest that well governed funds indeed outperform those worse governed by up to 1.5% a year. This result is manly driven by a significant underperformance of the poorly governed mutual funds. The well governed funds receive a performance with an alpha close to zero, which is apparently more than Fama and French (2010) have discovered for the average fund. [249, 250]

4.6.4   Linkages of the Morningstar Stewardship Rating to Mutual Fund Pattern

The literature regarding the Morningstar stewardship rating shows different results when questioning whether this rating in general is able to predict the future performance or the asset turnover. The literature also diverges in regard of the significance of single components in regard to future performance. But it could be stated that board quality and corporate culture seem to be most important. The manager's incentive component

---

[245] Cf. Fich/Shivdasani (2006) p. 689.

[246] Cf. Chou/Ng./Wang (2011) p. 1255.

[247] Cf. Chou/Ng./Wang (2011) p. 1254.

[248] This finding is consistent with the notion of educational networks between funds and stocks they are predominately invested in. Since the above mentioned study is more recent, I suggest that the potential benefits for funds by private information are no longer given.

[249] Cf. Chou/Ng./Wang (2011) p. 1266; Fama/French (2010).

[250] Please note that the underperformance of 1.38% per year in the time horizon of 1993 to 2006 stated by (Chou/Ng./Wang 2010) is not verifiable in (Fama/French 2010), but nevertheless the general pattern is indeed valid.

on the other hand is rather less relevant.[251] A further remark is that the entire literature regarding the Morningstar stewardship rating is based on a quite small sample size and a short time period and might therefore show only a limited reliability.

The overall stewardship grade and the portfolio turnover are constantly negative correlated. The correlation becomes stronger and is significant until the 80th quantile, thereafter the correlation effect decreases and is insignificant at the 90th quantile.[252] This seems rational since mutual funds with a high stewardship grade outperform those funds with a low stewardship grade by approximately 1.5% per year.[253]

Some interesting insights were gained by analyzing the significance of the single components used by the Morningstar stewardship rating. The board quality and corporate culture are most important components. The difference in alpha from well to badly governed mutual funds amounts each 1 to 1.5% annually, whereas the manager's incentives have only marginal impact or precisely in some quantiles.[254] Thus it seems that the corporate culture and board quality component gives valuable indications to which extent the fund management's interests align with investors' interests.[255]

The fee component is directly derived by the fee charged from investors. But nevertheless fees represent direct outflows to investors. This component shows no further explainable pattern in regard of fund performance and the portfolio turnover. This might also be due to the fact that Morningstar assigns the same fee score to different share classes of a fund.[256] Thus assigning scores for every share class might increase the significance and is also preferable from the investors' perspective, since the fees charged form investors might diverge substantially.[257]

A good governance or in more detail a good corporate culture is associated with a more stable and more reliable outcome. This is not only in interest of the investors but also in interest of the company (the mutual fund) itself. A less volatile performance offers fewer incentives to managers to increase risk in the purpose of recovering (potential) losses. And investors usually prefer those firms which show a more stable and reliable performance.[258][259]

---

[251] Cf. Chou/Ng./Wang (2011); Gottesman/Morey (2012); Wellman/Zhou (2008).

[252] Chen/Huang (2011) p. 323.

[253] Wellman/Zhou (2008) p. 1.

[254] Cf. Chou/Ng./Wang (2011) p. 1266.

[255] Cf. Chou/Ng./Wang (2011) p. 1266.

[256] Chen/Huang (2011) p. 320, 323, 326.

[257] For a further discussion see chapter 4.2.

[258] Cf. Sørensen (2002) p. 70 f..

In general a good corporate culture incorporates three different elements:

- A consensus of norms and behavior rules facilitates the detections of corporate wrongdoing and also prevent corporate wrongdoing.
- "Goal alignment" reduces the uncertainty in decision making and reduces potentially complicated debates.
- Enhanced motivation and thus effort, since employees feel that their actions are more valuable and that they are more independent.[260]

In that way the effect of the corporate culture component on performance and turnover seems to be less surprising, although it "only" describes how the management values the rights of their investors and the importance of the fiduciary duties to their investors.[261]

The effect of the board quality is somewhat surprising since the Morningstar definition is close to the SEC definition which only incorporate linkages between board members and investment advisors and the fund managers which are given by contracts. But they do not incorporate those resulting from familiarity. But nevertheless there are some evidences that the board quality component is able to predict the three factor mutual fund alpha.

The manager's incentive component on the other hand has a very small impact. This finding is hardly surprising since the two components: managerial holdings and the compensation structure included in manager incentives usually show reverse effects on the behavior of mutual fund managers. Even if Morningstar claims that an unfavorable structure, which focuses on the short run performance have a negative impact, the manager incentive score might be misleading.[262, 263] I suggest therefore that by splitting these two elements, their significance would be increased and they provide investors with a better advice.

Quite interesting is indeed the finding of the manager's incentive component. Overall, the manager's incentives are insignificant and positively correlated to performance. But when looking closer the manager's incentives in the right tail of the performance are

---

[259] This pattern should also on interest for mutual fund investors, since investors selecting funds with a volatile performance facing the risk buying on premium or discount which is quite unfavorable. This interest contradicts with the interests of mutual funds derived by the performance flow relation. For a further discussion see chapter 4.8.2.

[260] Cf. Gottesman/Morey (2012) p. 70; Sørensen (2002) p. 73.

[261] Cf. Chou/Ng./Wang (2011) p. 1266.

[262] Cf Morningstar Inc. (2010b) p. 2.

[263] For a more detailed discussion please see chapter 4.8.2 and chapter 4.8.3.

indeed significant.[264] This suggests that manager incentives, mutual fund holdings and a sustainable remuneration scheme are indeed effective, but only for already well performing mutual funds. In other words this finding suggests that those mutual funds with a high manager incentive score do not perform better than those with a low manager incentive score. But it could reject the assumption that mutual funds show on average a negative correlation between the manager incentive component and performance. Consequently, the level of performance is at least on average not linked to excessive risk assumption.

4.7 The Active Share of Mutual Funds

Mutual funds can only outperform their benchmark if the holdings are different from the benchmark. The deviation to the benchmark either originates by factor timing and/or stock picking ability. "Factor timing involves time-varying bets on systematic risk factors such as entire industries, sectors of the economy, or more generally any systematic risk relative to the benchmark index."[265] On the other hand, stock picking ability is presented by specifically selected single stocks.[266] In this case, it might be reasonable to assume that those funds, which extensively pick stocks are also those funds whose managers have good networks and thus predominately pick stocks.[267] It is interesting that funds show preferences for merely one of the two techniques. This finding makes it hard to estimate the active share.[268] The active share and the tracking error as well, are basically defined by the deviation to the benchmark index. The Tracking error can be calculated as follows:

$$R_{fund,t} - R_{f,t} = \alpha_{fund} - \beta_{fund}\left(R_{index,t} - R_{f,t}\right) + \varepsilon_{fund,t}$$

According to the formula above where $R_{fund,t}$ represents the return of the fund, $R_{index,t}$ the benchmark index and $R_{f,t}$ represent the return of the risk free rate. Maintaining a strong focus on the tracking error might be a problem, since the tracking error is hardly influenced by selective stock picking, whereas factor timing have substantially influence on the tracking error. This fact results that the tracking error of a portfolio, which selective picks stocks would usually (too) small. Consequently, the tracking error

---

[264] Chen/Huang (2011) p. 323.
[265] Cremers/Petajisto (2009) p. 3329.
[266] Cf. Cremers/Petajisto (2009) p. 3329.
[267] Cf. Cohen/Frazzini/Malloy (2008) p. 951f..
[268] Cf. Cremers/Petajisto (2009) p. 3330f., 3329f..

is not able to identify a stock picker. On the other hand, the tracking error is suitable to identify a factor timer.[269] The active share can be defined as:

$$Active\ Share = \frac{1}{2}\sum_{i=1}^{N} |w_{fund,i} - w_{index,i}|$$

$w_{fund,\ i}$ and $w_{index,I}$ represent the weights of the asset i in the fund portfolio and in the benchmark index. The relative weights of fund to the index are calculated thereby. An overweight in the fund relative to the index refers to **active long position**. In contrast, smaller or no holdings of a single stock relative to the benchmark refer to **active short position.** This portfolio contains 100% index holdings plus x% in short positions and in x% long positions. This long-short portfolio is used to measure the active management. Thus, the active share is "fraction of the portfolio that is different from (f)the benchmark index."[270,271] The usefulness of the active share is given by the fact that:

- Outperformance is only possible in cases where the fund's holdings deviate from the holdings of the index.
- This measure stands alone, hence it is not correlated and accordingly it can be combined with additional measures without facing the risk of correlations.[272]

The illustration below shows how stock picking and factor timing affects the exposure of mutual funds in regard to active share and the tracking error.

Different types of active and passive management

		Low	High
Active share high		Diversified stock picks	Concentrated stock picks
Active share low		Closet indexing	Factor bets
	Pure indexing		
0			
	0	Low	High
		Tracking error	

Illustration 2: Different types of active and passive management[273]

Apparently, combining the tracking error as the common measure of the activeness of a portfolio and the active share yields a good estimation about the source of the mutual funds success. In other words, is the mutual fund manager able to identify single stocks, (based on which information ever) or does the mutual fund prefers rather factor bets. A

---

[269] Cf. Cremers/Petajisto (2009) p. 3330f., 3334f..
[270] Cremers/Petajisto (2009) p. 3330.
[271] Cf. Cremers/Petajisto (2009) p. 3334f..
[272] Cf. Cremers/Petajisto (2009) p. 3330..
[273] Cf. Cremers/Petajisto (2009) p. 3331.

fund's active share is furthermore quite persistent. In combination with the fact that the active share allows taking inference on the future performance, causes that the active share is an interesting investment criteria.[274] Furthermore, mutual funds which show a change in their risk exposure and therefore, in their active share tend to performing worse. However, it is not entirely clear, whether these risk shifts are the result of a prior bad performance or if the manager "simply" wants to boost the fund performance. An unusual alternative might be that, at least as long as the fund management was not replaced, the change in the risk exposure is due to skill. [275]

The highest active share mutual funds outperform the benchmark before fees by annually 1.5% to 2.4%, which suggest stock picking skill. After controlling for fees and transaction costs, the benchmark is still outperformed by approximately 1.1% per year. Thus, even an unfavorable fee structure of some of these mutual funds is not able to take the share of this benefit.

On the other hand, those funds with the smallest active share generate a return of 0.1 to –0.6% relative to the benchmark. After controlling for fees and transaction costs, this number declines further from 1.4% to 1.8% annually. These alphas and the difference between the two alphas are statistically significant. The outperformance of a high active share is negative correlated to the fund size. Nevertheless, mutual funds, which are located in the two highest active share quintiles, still outperform the lowest active share quintiles by 1 to 2 percent per year.[276]

Mutual funds located in the highest active share quintile, show significant persistence in regard of benchmark adjusted performance. The persistence even holds when controlling for momentum. Looking merely at those funds, which are in the highest quintile of the prior year return funds and highest quintile active share funds results in a above benchmark return of above 5% before expenses and even 3.5% after expenses using Carharts' 1997 four-factor model.[277]

Furthermore, smaller funds tend to be more active than larger ones. In detail, the active share of mutual funds remain quite constant at nearly 70% until the fund reaches a volume of $1 billion. Subsequently. the active share declines to approximately 60% until the fund volume reaches a volume of $10 billion and then the active share declines

---

[274] Cf. Cremers/Petajisto (2009) p. 3329, 3331.
[275] Cf. Huang/Sialm./Zhang (2011) p. 2575.
[276] Cf. Cremers/Petajisto (2009) p. 3332.
[277] Cf. Cremers/Petajisto (2009) p. 3333.

to 50%.[278] Not surprisingly, since smaller funds have relative more investment opportunities than larger mutual funds and in addition, they face less liquidity constrains.[279]

Another important finding is that managers with a longer tenure show a higher active share.[280] This fact is consistent with the finding that managers with longer tenures might have more power due to empire building and thus are less tended to be fired.[281] These facts may result in a more active portfolio. Ranking mutual funds according to their performance in regard to their exposure to active share and tracking error this yields to:

1. The best performing mutual funds are **"concentrated stock picks"**, which have simultaneously a high active share and high tracking error. The tracking error in this case rather derived from strong selective stock picking than by factor bet.

2. The concentrated stock picks are followed by "**diversified stock pickers**" with a high active share and low tracking error.

3. Index funds or those mutual funds, which are close to the benchmark index with a low active share and a low tracking error, tend to perform badly as well: **"Closet indexing"**.

4. Funds with a low active share and a high tracking error, betting on (entirely) factors, tend to be performing worst: **"Factor bets"**.

The two top groups show some stock picking ability, but only the most active share funds are able to beat the benchmark.[282] This is consistent with the finding that only a very few funds generate a positive alpha.[283]

The benchmark adjusted return spread of former year winner and loser funds within the highest active share quintile amounts roughly 6.8% per year.[284] This spread might be induced by prior year losers, which were involved in excessive risk taking and therefore show a very high active share without equivalent skill.[285] A complementary explanation might be that these managers are simply lucky stock picker even without any skills.[286]

The percentage of funds with a high active share has declined from 40% in 1980 to roughly 2% in the year 2003. This outcome is in line with an increase in the percentage

---

[278] Cf. Cremers/Petajisto (2009) p. 3342.
[279] Cf. Pollet/Wilson (2008) p. 2941 f..
[280] Cf. Cremers/Petajisto (2009) p. 3345.
[281] Cf. Ding/Wermers (2012) p. 4.
[282] Cf. Cremers/Petajisto (2009) p. 3351.
[283] Cf. Barras/Scaillet/Wermers (2010) p. 181f.; Kosowski, et al. (2006) p. 2575.
[284] Cf. Cremers/Petajisto (2009) p. 3354.
[285] Cf. Massa/Patgiri (2007) p. 1777.
[286] Cf. Kosowski, et al. (2006) p. 2554.

of mutual funds which show no skill at all since only mutual funds with a high active share are able o outperform the benchmark.[287]

4.8   Incentives in Mutual Funds

4.8.1   A Brief Overview

Incentives play an important role when analyzing the behavior of any individual and organization. In mutual funds these incentives have, at least partially, strong influence on performance and on the risk taking behavior of the management.[288] Some incentives are explicitly given, for example by the fee structure, the remuneration scheme of board members and managers and by their holdings in the mutual funds as well.[289] The last point is rather voluntary than mandatory.[290] Other incentives are inherent in the mutual fund market and rather implicitly given.[291] Career concerns and the fear of dismissals are also important aspects directly linked to mutual fund managers, especially to the younger ones.[292] The performance flow relation and the tendency of (some) investors to be disposition prone represents also incentives for the fund management.[293] In general, it can be assumed that individuals and therefore organizations are interested in maximizing their personal wealth and utility.[294] This structure might be used and to "guide" managers. As already stated above when talking about fees and the affiliation to banks, these incentives are not necessarily advantageous for investors because they may result in excessive risk taking behavior.[295]

4.8.2   Fees and the Manager Compensation Schemes

Mutual fund advisors usually generate revenues from the ongoing fees calculated as a percentage of AuM, which provides incentives to increase the AuM. Fund managers work as employees of the advisory firm, but the structure of their individual contracts is kept usually undisclosed and can only be evaluated by surveys. Studies support the hypothesis that the managerial compensation is closely linked to the performance

---

[287] Cf. Cremers/Petajisto (2009) p. 3347; Kosowski, et al. (2006) p. 2554.
[288] See for example: Farnsworth/Taylor (2006); Khorana/Servaes/Wedge (2007b).
[289] Cf. Chevalier/Ellison (1997) p. 1167; Davis/Payne/McMahan (2007) p. 330; Evans. (2008) p. 513.
[290] Cf Khorana/Servaes/Wedge (2007b) p. 183 f..
[291] Cf. Brown/Harlow/Strakes (1996) p. 85.
[292] Cf. Chevalier/Ellison (1999b) p. 390 - 391 f..
[293] Cf. Chevalier/Ellison (1997) p. 1169; Huang/Sialm./Zhang (2011) p. 2576.
[294] Cf. Matsumura/Shin (2005) p. 102.
[295] Cf, Massa/Patgiri (2007) p. 1777.

respective to the assets under management.[296] Beneath this, the vast majority of compensation is also linked to the overall performance of the fund family or even the affiliated financial conglomerate. This linkage is plausible since it motivates managers to share their expertise and knowledge which should be in the shareholders' interest.[297] Nevertheless, as already stated in the chapter about bank affiliation,[298] mutual fund managers might be motivated or even forced to act predominantly in the interest of the advisor or the fund family instead in the interest of the fund investors.

The importance of the performance for mutual funds and thus mutual fund managers is heavily linked to the investors' performance flow sensitivity. The higher this sensitivity is, the higher the incentives of managers to perform well, since a bad performance would result in net outflows.[299] Since a good performance in the past has significant influence on future fund flows, managers have apparently incentives to perform well. Especially in the US, managers have furthermore strong incentives that their mutual fund will be among the top group (four or five star Morningstar rated), since only those funds receive net inflows. These incentives cause that managers of funds which are close to their peer group's top rating, tend to take inappropriate high risks to receive the next best rating scale. This would result in higher AuM and higher compensations. Unfortunately, investors might be harmed in this case. For example, managers in three star rated funds have incentives to boost fund performance and receive four stars. Managers who manage four stars rated funds have generally incentives to boost performance until they receive five stars as well. A decline to a three stars rating causes massive outflows and the mutual fund would be harmed. Otherwise, four stars rated funds still receive high inflows. Especially former five stars rated fund managers might be consequently quite risk averse, since higher risks in this case may cause a drop in performance and thus significant outflows. The behavior of five stars rated funds is in the same line , since excessive risk cause advantageous.[300] The fact that fund advisors are remunerated by a percentage of AuM creates a strong incentive for those to focus on an asset growth. In combination with the performance flow pattern, especially of retail investors, it leads to some serious problems for investors. Hence, fund families have therefore incentives to run "only" top performing funds and worst performing funds,

---

[296] Cf. Farnsworth/Taylor (2006) p. 306; Khorana/Servaes/Wedge (2007) p. 183.
[297] Cf. Farnsworth/Taylor (2006) p. 306.
[298] See chapter 4.5.
[299] Cf. Christoffersen/Musto (2002) p. 1499f.; Matsumura/Shin (2005) p. 107.
[300] Cf. Chevalier/Ellison. (1997) p. 1168 - 1170; Del Guercio/Tkac (2008) p. 928 f.; Qiu (2003) p. 164.

instead to rather medium performers.[301] This is based on the notion that top performers attract high inflows, whereas weak performing funds do not suffer from equivalent outflows at least when looking on retail funds.[302]

A counterforce might be given due to career concerns of mutual fund managers. As long as the excess performance is positive, the termination risk hardly changes, whereas a negative excess performance causes a steep increase in the risk of termination.[303] In addition, the performance flow relation give some incentives to play save. This fact applies in particular for worse performing mutual funds, since the benefits of increased risk are only marginal, whereas the potential drawbacks might cause that the manager is worse of.

4.8.3 Holdings of Mutual Fund Managers and Board Members

Another possibility avoiding excessive risk taking induced by the remuneration scheme, are the holdings of managers as well as holdings of board members in the mutual fund they manage or overview. These holdings have to be disclosed assigned to the different holding classes build on the personal assets invested in the fund.[304] In both cases, an increase in holdings is associated with an increase in performance and a better alignment with the investors' interests. Holdings of board members lead to a better monitoring of the mutual fund managers.

Consequently, if board members have low or even no ownership in the fund or fund family those funds significantly underperform the benchmark by around 2 to 2.5% annually.[305] Board member holdings are especially important for bigger funds, since these funds are pronounced in particular to diseconomies of scale and thus a good board is essential to keep the costs low. Furthermore, a good alignment with the shareholders interests' is only given when these holdings are large.[306] Funds whose board independent members have no or only low holding in the fund are also associated with a higher expense ratio. Generally, there is a negative relation between board holding s and the expense ratio.[307]

---

[301] Cf. Gaspar/Massa/Matos (2006) p. 74.
[302] Cf. Del Guercio/Tkac (2001) p. 37.
[303] Cf. Chevalier/Ellison. (1999b) p. 391; Nohel/Wang/Zheng (2010) p. 2343.
[304] Cf. Cremers et al. (2009) p. 1355; Khorana/Servaes/Wedge (2007b) p. 180.
[305] Cf. Cremers et al. (2009) p. 1360.
[306] Cf. Cremers et al. (2009) p. 1364 - 1366.
[307] Cf. Cremers et al. (2009) p. 1370.

Manager holdings show a positive correlation to future fund performance as well.[308] Moreover, when looking on the non-mutual fund linked literature there is some evidence that managerial holdings are negatively related to white-collar crimes.[309] 50% of mutual fund managers have only small or no holdings in the funds they manage. An increase in holdings of one basis point of the AuM is associated with an increase in performance of three basis points. In addition, managerial holdings are largest in those funds, which have performed well in the past, have lower front end loads, in funds with longer manager tenure, in funds affiliated to a smaller family and in smaller funds.[310] The fund size might be the only reason why holdings are bigger in smaller funds, since an absolute equal large amount counts more in a smaller fund. Indeed, it is also possible that managers invested in those funds expect higher future returns and therefore invest in these funds. The fact that holdings are positively correlated to the manager tenure is more complicate to analyze. On the one hand, it is possible that the managerial holdings have simply accumulated during the holding period. On the other hand, it is also possible that this finding is linked to a good governance structure in general, since those funds might encourage or even force their managers to invest in the funds they manage.[311]

The positive correlation of manager holdings and the subsequent performance might be due to superior information, which seems unlikely, especially when looking at the findings of (e.g. Fama and French 2010 or Hereil et al. 2010). Alternatively, a participation in the fund might causes incentives for managers. These incentives may result in a higher effort and especially less excessive risk taking, which consequently results in a higher performance. The results persist even after controlling some cross-sectional variation linked to the fund, fund family and manager characteristics.[312] Nevertheless, regardless of the source of this superior performance, managerial holdings are a valuable indicator for investor when searching for funds.

---

[308] Cf. Khorana/Servaes/Wedge (2007b) p. 179 ff.
[309] Cf. Schnatterly (2003) p. 606.
[310] Cf. Khorana/Servaes/Tufano (2007b) p. 179, 181.
[311] Cf. Sørensen, (2002) p. 73.
[312] Cf. Khorana/Servaes/Tufano (2007b) p. 182.

4.8.4 Mutual Funds and Window Dressing

Window dressing represents a drawback, which becomes even worse because (retail) investors are not able to uncover these actions before they occur. Thus, they would be able to redeem their shares, since some mutual funds have to report their holdings only one time a year.[313] In the US, mutual funds are required to disclose the holdings two times a year, whereas some funds, even if not required, disclose their holdings four times a year.[314]

A more frequently discloser of holdings causes transparency. High transparency is in general considered as positive, since it reduces the chances for fund managers to window dress their portfolio. However, this transparency can also cause a decline in performance of top performing mutual funds, in so far other investors may "front-run" and imitate the fund holdings. Especially on a less liquid market the superior performance might destroy. On the other hand, transparency has a disciplinary effect on mutual funds, since investors may redeem funds, if the assets hold by the fund may be unbalanced, too risky or maybe unethical.[315] It should be obvious, that managers are nevertheless able to hide most of their holdings and actions due to "window dressing".[316]

Even though holdings data is provided, it seems questionable if (retail) investors are able to analyze the information. The analysis is getting more complicated, since fund managers have incentives to window-dress their portfolio holdings. Reasons for window dressing are e.g. that managers of outperforming funds want to hide their actual holdings in order to prevent other funds from mirroring their strategy.[317] Additionally, managers in worse performing funds have incentives to shift returns from one period to another by purchasing stocks they have already invested in at the last minutes of the end of a period and selling these stocks at the beginning of the following one. This practice is known as "painting the tape" and is basically illegal.[318] Window dressing also takes place by purchasing more "appropriate" or selling less "appropriate" stocks to "fine-tune" the portfolio for accounting and reporting purposes.[319] The performance-induced

---

[313] For example in the Netherlands: see Palomino,/Uhlig (2007) p. 53)

[314] Cf. Kacperczyk/Sialm/Zheng (2006) p. 2384; Palomino,/Uhlig (2007) p. 53.

[315] Cf. Frank et al. (2004) p. 516 f..

[316] A positive example for transparency is given by the ETF segment of the Deutsche Bank. The collateral of their swap based ETFs is disclosed with a time lag of only a few days. However, these funds do not face the risk of front running. See for example: Deutsche Asset & Wealth Management (2013).

[317] Cf. Kacperczyk/Sialm/Zheng (2006) p. 2381; Meier/Schaumburg (2006) p. 2.

[318] Cf. Carhart et al. (2002) p. 661 f; Meier/Schaumburg (2006) p. 1 f..

[319] Cf. Brown/Harlow/Strakes (1996) p. 93.

window dressing is most predominately for funds, which have also strong incentives due to a strong performance flow relation of their investors.[320] In addition, trading over a short period of time is costly, but do not generate benefits for investors.[321] Beneath the financial impact, investors are also harmed by a misleading performance and holdings. Even when retail investors uncover these actions, it is questionable if they would (consequently) vote with their feet and redeem the shares because they face search costs and are disposition prone in the way retail investors face vicious circle and take. It might become even worse, when marketing oriented funds are involved in such actions.[322]

4.8.5 Return Transfers in Mutual Fund Families

Fund families with different fee structures, maybe even hedge funds and mutual funds represent another incentive, basically originating in the fact that retail investors are disposition prone and rather unsophisticated. Besides the phenomenon that funds offer different share classes,[323] fund families transfer profits from low value to high value funds. High value funds are those funds generating high value for the fund family by higher expense ratios or fees in general. The purpose of such actions is to increase the overall fund family profitability instead of improving the profitability of a single mutual fund.[324]

These actions are possible due to the fact that 80% of the assets under management are invested in fund families offering more than one fund and thus managers tend to work rather for the fund family than for a single fund. Return transfers are build on the fact that the profit of the fund family is directly linked to the fees charged and thus on the assets under management in the funds. Furthermore, investors react disproportionally to a good performance in the past.[325] These actions are executed in three different forms:

- Performance is transferred to high fee funds on the expense of low fee funds.

- Currently well performing funds (in the current year) are supported on the expense of low performing ones.

---

[320] Cf. Carhart et al. (2002) p. 666.
[321] Cf. Meier/Schaumburg (2006) p. 3.
[322] Cf. Sirri/Tufano (1998) p. 1589.
[323] See chapter 4.2.2.
[324] Cf. Gaspar/Massa/Matos (2006) p. 73.
[325] Cf. Cici/Gibson/Moussawi (2010) p. 169; Gaspar/Massa/Matos (2006) p. 73.

- Younger funds are supported on the expense of older funds, since younger funds receive relatively higher inflows for a good past performance than older ones.[326]

The performance differs between high and low value funds up to 3.3% annually. Such actions are more likely in times where the low value funds perform well and high value funds perform relatively worse. In addition, large fund families, which offer many and diversified funds are more likely to be involved in such actions.[327] These actions take place via two forms of trades. First, preferential allocation describes that the best deals are preferential for high value funds and second, opposite trades. This describes a pattern, where the fund family coordinates the trades in a way that low value funds buffer the price pressure induced by the trades of high value funds or the funds even trade within the family "without" using the open market.[328]

4.8.6 Side-by-Side Management of Mutual Funds and Hedge Funds

Side-by-side management of mutual funds and hedge funds represents a similar situation like the above mentioned. Such constellations are important to know, as it is commonly assumed that hedge fund managers are more skilled than mutual fund managers. Therefore, searching for a hedge fund manager who also manages a mutual fund might result in a superior performance of the mutual fund. This notion is proved by the fact that those mutual fund managers outperform their peers even before the hedge fund was initiated. Reasons why mutual funds are willing to accept these side-by-side deals are that they can attract and retain star performers.[329] However, the effect on mutual fund performance differs substantially depending on whether this side-by-side management is defined on the family level or on the manager level. These two constellations are interesting, since the managers have contracts with different agents, namely the hedge fund and the mutual fund. In addition, the manager should keep in mind the fiduciary duties of the shareholders. This special kind of double agency causes some incentives to use the incentives provided by hedge fund properties and thus harming investors in such mutual funds.[330] Side-by-side managers lay a strong focus on small cap stocks and momentum stocks.[331] In cases where side-by-side management is

---

[326] Cf. Chevalier/Ellison (1997) p. 1177 - 1179; Gaspar/Massa/Matos (2006) p. 75.
[327] Cf. Gaspar/Massa/Matos (2006) p. 75.
[328] Cf. Gaspar/Massa/Matos (2006) p. 76.
[329] Cf. Nohel/Wang/Zheng (2010) p. 2342, 2362.
[330] Cf. Nohel/Wang/Zheng (2010) p. 2343.
[331] Cf. Nohel/Wang/Zheng (2010) p. 2353.

defined on the family level, the picture is similar as it stated above.[332] Looking merely at the manager level, side-by-side management results in a substantial and significant outperforms of comparable mutual funds of 1 to 1.6% annually, whereas the hedge fund only performs on average with his peers. The differing performance in these two cases might partly be induced due to different samples.[333] In cases, where the side-by-side management is defined on the fund family level these actions are most prevalent in mutual funds. Those mutual funds, which have similar investment objectives as the hedge fund underperform comparable mutual funds by up to 1.5% annually. This underperformance is based on a reduced participation in underpriced IPO contributions, which represents a similar situation like the preferential allocation as already stated above. The underperformance when defining side-by-side management on the family level amounted on average approximately 0.5% annually before and after fees.[334] The superior stock picking ability, if it exists, is faded away by unfavorable favoritism of hedge fund (managers) at the expense of mutual fund investors by the fund management or the fund family, respective or other factors not captured.[335]

4.8.7   A behavior perspective on Incentives

Many incentives discussed above, are funded on the fact that some investors are unsophisticated and disposition prone. This fact is relevant for sophisticated investors and thus mutual funds itself.[336] This behavior pattern is widely explainable regarding the utility function developed in the prospect theory by Kahneman and Tversky in 1979. The theory explains why it is possible that managers which have performed badly in the past are quite interested to increases the risk proportion of their portfolio.[337] Individuals basically are more risk-averse in regard to loosing their gains. Such a behavior is founded in the idea that individuals feel regret in cases they face losses and pride in cases of gains. Moreover, individual investors and (fund manager) are averse in realizing losses since that would admitting their (wrong) personal judgment. This behavior becomes increasingly prevalent explaining the (personal) error to others. Hence individuals tend to realize gains too early and hold losers too long. Interestingly, selling a stock "too" early which continues rising causes that regret since a potential

---

[332] Cf. Cici/Gibson/Moussawi (2010) p. 169.
[333] Cf. Nohel/Wang/Zheng (2010) p. 2345 f..
[334] Cf. Cici/Gibson/Moussawi (2010) p. 169 - 171; Gaspar/Massa/Matos (2006) p. 76.
[335] Cf. Cici/Gibson/Moussawi (2010) p. 171.
[336] Cf. Cici, G. (2012) p. 795.
[337] Cf. Kahneman/Tversky (1979) p. 279.

gain is lost.[338] Furthermore, individuals are sometimes overconfident. Consequently, they are, overoptimistic about the future development of their investments and hence reluctant in loss realization. It is interesting to know that this kind of behavior cannot be ruled out by an implementation of incentives or "calibration". [339] It becomes worse in a situation where individuals throwing "good money after bad" money which describes a situation where additional assets where invested in loosing stocks.[340]

One possible way avoiding such problems might be the use of stop-loss orders. The main advantage of such orders are: they are defined previously and they are executed automatically.[341, 342]

4.9   A Cross-sectional View on Hedge Funds

Regarding the impact of incentives and manager characteristics in the asset management business is provided by hedge funds. Hedge funds and mutual funds are different. In contrast to mutual funds, hedge fund managers charge 15% up to 20% of the funds profits as bonus after exceeding a certain level of performance.[343] This model might be a source of excessive risk taking.[344] however, at the same time hedge fund managers usually have substantial amounts of their personal wealth invested in the fund. Furthermore, in some cases these managers are even partners, accordingly their personal wealth get hurt in cases when the hedge fund performs worse or gets bankrupt. Mutually properties of mutual funds and hedge fund are an expense ratio of one to two percent of the assets under management. [345] The large stakes of personal wealth of managers in hedge fund also cause that funds have less incentives to force on the growth of assets under management. Consequently, hedge funds are more likely to be closed for new investors and thus protecting fund performance for diseconomies of scale, which is quite uncommon in case of mutual funds.[346]

---

[338] Cf. Shefrin/Statma (1985) p. 781 f..

[339] Cf. Tversky/Kahneman (1992) p. 1127 f..

[340] Cf. Shefrin/Statma (1985) p. 789.

[341] Cf. Shefrin/Statma (1985) p. 783.

[342] This situation is well described by the following statement of a trader, which is quoted by (Shefrin/Statma (1985) p. 783) "I have a hard and fast rule that I never let my losses on a trade exceed ten percent. Say I buy a ten-dollar stock. As soon as it goes to nine dollars, I must sell it and take a loss. [...] The traders who get wiped out hope against hope. I've seen a good hundred come and go since I've been here in 1964. They're stubborn. They refuse to take losses ... When you're breaking in a new trader, the hardest thing to learn is to admit that you're wrong. It's a hard pill to swallow. You have to be man enough to admit to your peers that you're wrong and get out. Then you're alive and playing the game the next day."

[343] Cf. Ackermann/MacEnally/Ravenscraft (1999) p. 833 f.; Li/Zhang/Zhao (2011) p. 60.

[344] Cf Massa/Patgiri (2007) p. 1777.

[345] Cf. Ackermann/MacEnally/Ravenscraft (1999) p. 833 f.; Li/Zhang/Zhao (2011) p. 60.

[346] Cf. Ackermann/MacEnally/Ravenscraft (1999) p. 835.

An investment in a hedge fund is usually only possible when investing higher amounts. Hedge funds have a so called lock-up period this describes a time period where investors are not able to redeem their assets.[347] Mutual fund investors are able to purchase and redeem shares virtually at every day with only small minimum investments. Some mutual funds charge back-end fees and thus give incentives for longer holding periods.[348] Hedge fund investors are assumed to be more sophisticated, which is reflected by a more symmetric performance flow relation. Furthermore, hedge funds are widely unregulated and investments in a hedge fund are seen, as an investment in the manager's talent, since the hedge fund manager has more influence on performance as in a mutual fund.[349]

---

[347] Cf. Ackermann/MacEnally/Ravenscraft (1999) p. 835.
[348] Cf. Smith (2010b) p. 52 f..
[349] Cf, Ackermann/MacEnally/Ravenscraft (1999) p. 834; Li/Zhang/Zhao (2011) p. 63.

5 Mutual Fund Selection

5.1 What Investors Really Do? – Is Such a Behavior Rational?

Mutual fund investors focus on past performance or ratings, like the Morningstar star rating when buying mutual funds. As the Morningstar star rating is based on past performances, aforementioned investors consequently chase, more or less extensively, past performance.[350] At the same time only the most sophisticated investors react on past performance or bad news by redeeming their shares:[351] Thus investors show strong asymmetric reactions towards good and worse performance of mutual funds. This pattern seems even more astonishing, since performance persists only over short horizons.[352] Especially for those investors following a buy-and-hold strategy, such biased behavior might be quite costly. Moreover, retail investors even show momentum in their investment decisions.[353] This raises the question whether these investors really know what they are buying, or whether they are "simply" following brokerage or bank's advices, or whether they are bounded in saving plans.[354]

More astonishing is that even institutional investors are exposed to the disposition effect.[355] These investors should indeed be aware of such irrational behavioral tendencies and consequently implement some internal regulations and requirements to minimize the consequences of such actions.[356]

In addition (retail) investors seem to underestimate or even ignore the expense ratios when purchasing funds. This behavior is especially surprising, since costs represent a predictable asset outflow and a deadweight loss.[357] In some cases (e. g. index mutual funds) the expense ratio is the only criteria left. But even in this case sophisticated retail investors fail to select the right mutual fund.[358] This pattern becomes even worse in cases where investors have bought a mutual fund with (high) end-loads fees. Because this high fees hinder investors to switch their assets in another fund, as end-loads are a deadweight loss. Furthermore small investors face relatively higher search costs, which additionally hinder to switch their assets into another mutual fund.[359]

---

[350] Cf. Del Guercio/Tkac (2001) p.37; Del Guercio/Tkac (2008) p. 918.
[351] Cf. Jank (2010) p. 2, 12.
[352] Cf. Blake/Morey (2000) p. 467.; Brown/Goetzmann (1995) p. 691 - 693; Carhart (1993) p. 57; Hendricks/Patel/Zeckhauser (1993) p. 93.
[353] Cf. Jank (2010) p. 3.
[354] Cf. Knuutila/Puttonen/Smythe (2007) p. 89.
[355] Cf. Jank (2010) p. 13.
[356] Cf. Shefrin/Statma (1985) p. 781 f
[357] Cf. Choi/Laibson/Madrian (2010) p. 1406 f.; Houge /Wellman (2006) p. 2,
[358] Cf. Choi/Laibson/Madrian (2010) p. 1406 f..
[359] Cf. Adams/Mansi/Nishikawa (2012) p. 2246; Jank/Wedow. (2010) p. 2.

The inability of individuals to react equally to good and poor performance and the fact that (retail) investors are unable to incorporate the costs provides strong incentives for mutual fund families to use this pattern for their own purposes. For example, these incentives result in mutual funds offering multiple share class funds with an unfavorable fee structure especially in those funds with front-end loads which are predominately demanded by the most unsophisticated investors.[360]

Furthermore and even worse for investors is the fact that mutual fund families have incentives to play on the disposition effect, while offering mutual funds only in the performance extremes instead of medium performing mutual funds. This effect may be even more severe when mutual funds are involved in return transfers within mutual fund families.[361]

When evaluating this behavior, it can hardly assigned as rational, even if the disposition effect, as well as the underestimation of the expense ratio is a part of the human mental behavior and rather subconscious.

Against this background, the findings of a recent study are indeed desirable. This study has found that, in addition to these rather quantitative factors, mutual fund investors also incorporate the Morningstar stewardship rating, which considers qualitative factors which are usually quite persistent.[362] This behavior is basically desirable, since a good governance rating is associated with many positive effects for investors.[363] Nevertheless investors should be careful while using this rating. Concerns are founded in the fact the stewardship rating is highly condensed and partly uses factors which might have reverse effects, or is only significant at the right tail of the performance.[364]

As conclusion, the currently used criteria in the mutual fund selection are rather inferior than superior, since investors systematically fail to select those mutual funds which perform well in the future. Hence, investors should look at other criteria, which more persistent or which allow them to derive the superior future performance, ideally in the long run.

---

[360] Cf. Adams/Mansi/Nishikawa (2012) p. 2245; Houge /Wellman (2006) p. 27; Nanda/Wang/Zheng (2009) p. 329 f.
[361] Cf. Gaspar/Massa/Matos (2006) p. 73 – 75.
[362] Cf. Morningstar Inc. (2010b) p. 1 f.; Wellman/Zhou (2008) p.1.
[363] Cf. Chou/Ng./Wang (2011) p. 1254.
[364] Cf. Chen/Huang (2011) p. 323;Cremers et al. (2009) p. 1360. Farnsworth/Taylor (2006) p. 306; Khorana/Servaes/Wedge (2007) p. 183; Morningstar Inc. (2010b) p. 1 f..

5.2   Alternative Criteria in the Mutual Fund Selection

5.2.1   The Purpose and Functionality of Alternative Criteria

Alternative strategies aim to identify those mutual funds which are likely to outperform the market or at least the average peers by other factors than luck. More recent studies analyzing mutual funds try to find additional pattern in mutual funds which are persistent over longer horizons and which have impact on the future mutual fund performance.[365] In applicable cases mutual fund investors could use these criteria and buy respective sell these funds.

Those alternative criteria usually use past performance as an additional criterion rather as the main investment criterion. These criteria basically are[366]:

- Load fees and expense ratio
- The active share of the mutual fund portfolios
- Governance linked criteria

5.2.2   The Fee and Expense Ratio

The fee and expense ratio should be the most important investment criterion for mutual fund investors, because these costs represent a reliable asset outflow for investors. This might be avoidable in many cases. In addition higher fees are rather a signal for weak governance and inferior performance than vice versa.[367] Even more important, a study located in Denmark suggests that investors following solely a cost-based rating are able to generate a superior performance. In more detail: Investors buying low cost mutual funds are able to outperform those buying high costs funds by up to 4 percent per year. More interesting especially for retail investors is the fact that this outperformance especially holds in the long run (eight to ten years).[368]

An interesting criterion when looking at the load fee structure might be conditional back-end fees, which only apply for short term investors, since the remaining investors are harmed by extensive trading activities[369]. Thus this structure would prevent investors from excessive trading, but this also limits the investor itself.

---

[365] Cf. Bechmann/Rangvid (2007); Chen/Huang (2011); Cremers/Petajisto (2009).
[366] Cf. Before applying these criteria the investor already knows in which market she wants to invest.
[367] Cf. Ding/Wermers (2012) p. 6; Mehran/Stulz (2007) p. 271.
[368] Cf. Bechmann/Rangvid (2007) p. 662 - 664.
[369] Cf. Smith (2010b) p.52 f..

5.2.3 The Active Share of Mutual fund Portfolios

The active share is an interesting criterion for investors, since it allows investors to take inference about the deviation of the mutual fund portfolio to its benchmark. Moreover the active share can be seen as a proxy of the managers' talent. Investors should invest their assets predominately in those mutual funds which are in the two active share top groups: the diversified stock pickers and concentrated stock picks.[370] Thus the tracking error should also be used be differentiate between those two. Combining these measures with the prior year performance yields a quite reliable forecast for a superior performance in the current year.[371]

5.2.4 Governance Linked Criteria

The governance structure of mutual funds allows investors to derive some rather soft but nevertheless important facts of the mutual funds. The academic literature suggests that especially the corporate culture and the board quality, both incorporated in the Morningstar stewardship rating, are quite valuable for investors.[372]

The corporate culture allows investors to take inference how serious the mutual fund (family) takes the fiduciary duties. Furthermore, a good corporate culture has influence on the entire mutual fund, even when some advantage like the reduced likelihood of the participation in white collar crimes are rather theoretically, it is nevertheless valuable.[373]

The board quality is especially important, since it incorporates the holdings of board members which leads to a better alignment with the investors' interests. This results in a better monitoring of the mutual fund management and the advisory firm, respectively. Whether the independency of the board members is important remains an open question, since in many cases there are linkages between the fund management and the board, but the board members are also treated as independent.[374]

Manager holdings and the remuneration / fee structure are important, too. Unfortunately, the manager incentive score of the Morningstar stewardship rating incorporates both elements, which might deteriorate the value of this element.[375] Nevertheless, investors should look especially on the managerial holdings. The reason is that the higher the manager's holdings in a mutual fund are, the less likely will she bear

---

[370] Cf. Cremers/Petajisto (2009) p. 3331, 3351.
[371] Cf. Cremers/Petajisto (2009) p. 3354.
[372] Cf. Chou/Ng./Wang (2011) p. 1266.
[373] Cf. Morningstar Inc. (2010b) p. 2; Schnatterly (2003) p. 587; Cf. Sørensen (2002) p. 70 f..
[374] Cf. Kuhnen (2009) p. 2188; Morningstar Inc. (2010b) p. 2
[375] Cf. Cremers et al. (2009) p. 1364 - 1366; Morningstar Inc. (2010b) p. 2.

excessive risks and the less abusive actions are they expected to take.[376] Composing the remuneration scheme and fee structure is more complicated, since it is very important to look at the fund family and in some cases to look at the affiliated financial institution. A fund's affiliation to an (investment) bank or to a publicly held fund family usually causes a strong conflict of interest, which is usually harmful for mutual fund investors.[377]

The overall stewardship rating grade has nevertheless some value for investors, since those mutual funds with a superior rating tend to invest in better governed stocks. Moreover, those mutual funds are endowed with an alpha indistinguishable from zero, which is at least better than the average mutual fund.[378]

5.2.5 Selecting a Mutual Fund

As presented above there are some valuable criteria for fund investors. Most important when selecting mutual funds are the costs associated with the funds, especially because the costs are easily observable and predictable and consequently easily avoidable. The active share mutual funds are on special interest, since the active share represents how strong the mutual fund selective picks stocks. Combining these with the fund performance it also allows investors to anticipate the success of the management in the future. When incorporating also governance-related patterns, investors are further able to focus on those mutual funds which are less likely to be involved in abusive actions and those which are likely to harm their investors. In addition to that, investors should use stop-loss orders to minimize the impact of the disposition effect.

But regardless which criteria are used, it should be mentioned that investors in active strategies / mutual funds always face the risk that the management is only able to generate a true zero alpha. Even worse: The risk remains that the management is indeed unskilled, resulting in a negative alpha. Thus investors should think carefully whether they want to face the risk linked to an active strategy. In recent years this question has gained importance, due to the fact that index funds and also ETFs are widely available. Both strategies are passive which means that investors do not have to remunerate an expensive but "worthless" active management.

---

[376] Cf. Khorana/Servaes/Wedge (2007b) p. 179 ff.; Schnatterly (2003) p. 606.
[377] Cf. Cf. Davis/Payne/McMahan (2007) p. 323.
[378] Cf. Chou/Ng./Wang (2011) p. 1254.

6 Conclusion

In this study I analyzed which criteria are used by investors when selecting mutual funds and which criteria should be used. For this purpose I analyzed the behavior of mutual fund investors as well as the characteristics and the behavior of mutual funds itself. I assume that investors who decides to invest in active mutual funds aim to outperform a passive alternative, since the passive alternative is much easier to find and shows usually fewer risks.

While analyzing the behavior of mutual fund investors, it becomes apparent that they strongly focus on past performance. Chasing past performance is not essentially an inferior strategy, since fund performance shows some momentum. This strategy becomes risky as most investors obviously seem to ignore the fund's past performance when redeeming it. Even more extreme, investors tend to sell predominately winning funds and while holding the losing funds too long.

A further key finding of this study is that investors obviously seem to underestimate or even ignore other also important criteria. These are for example the costs associated with mutual funds, governance issues or the active share of mutual funds.

The underestimation of expenses and load fees is interesting, because these costs have a direct negative impact on investors' return. Furthermore, they are disclosed in any prospectus and hence investors can easily receive a higher return by avoiding those funds.

Governance criteria in the selection of mutual funds especially by retail investors turn out to have little impact. The reason for that might be that this investor clientele are not professionally enough to understand the importance of governance criteria. But the market timing scandals might increase the awareness of these criteria even for retail investors.

The active share is an interesting criterion for investors, since it allows concluding the stock picking skill of mutual fund managers. Furthermore funds with a high active share outperform those with a low active share significantly, especially when adding superior past performance.

The last two criteria require some extensive research and hence are rather suitable for professional investors or rating provider.

In addition it becomes apparent that, mutual fund (families) take advantage of investors' behavior. Such harmful actions are most prevalent in fund families which are affiliated to a bank or which are publicly held. At least some of these drawbacks might be eliminable by buying funds with a superior stewardship rating and by implementing stop-loss orders.

Moreover, it becomes apparent that the purchase decisions of mutual fund investors strongly depend on their financial sophistication and the distribution channel. In Europe the vast majority of mutual funds are distributed via banks, hence those funds with linkages to banks show a much weaker performance flow compared to those not affiliated to banks. Even worse is the fact that those mutual funds in Europe are usually more expensive than mutual funds not linked to banks.

The above stated patterns suggest that some investors do not understand the basic functionalities of mutual funds and hence "simply" following the advice of their bankers.

It should be mentioned that there are indeed some other valuable criteria or strategies for the mutual fund selection. Taking this study's limited scope and coverage into consideration, the above mentioned criteria represent a subjective choice.

Moreover, especially regarding the sources of superior performance, there is much research to be done. This is due to the reason that the literature usually captures "only" one small aspect without incorporating other aspects. I would suggest a study based on a bootstrap analysis. This study may include various factors, like the bank affiliation, the educational networks of the fund management, the remuneration structure, whether the fund family is publicly held and a time component to test whether these factors have changed and if when, which seem apparent when looking at some other studies.

Concluding this study:

Investors in active mutual fund might be able to outperform a passive strategy. Nevertheless, this seems only possible with some afford and a rather active than a buy-and-hold strategy, since mutual funds extensively using unsophisticated behavior.

7 References

Ackermann, C./MacEnally, R./Ravenscraft, D. (1999): The performance of hedge funds: Risk, return, and incentives, in: Journal of Finance, Vol. 54, p. 833–874.

Adams, J. C./Mansi, S. A./Nishikawa, T. (2012): Are mutual fund fees excessive?, in: Journal of Banking & Finance, Vol. 36, p. 2245–2259.

Antypas, A./Caporale, G. M./Kourogenis, N./Pittis, N. (2009): Selectivity, Market Timing and the Morningstar Star-Rating System, in: SSRN Electronic Journal.

Baker, M./Litov, L./Wachter, J. A./Wurgler, J. (2010): Can Mutual Fund Managers Pick Stocks? Evidence from Their Trades Prior to Earnings Announcements, in: Journal of Financial and Quantitative Analysis, Vol. 45, p. 1111–1131.

Barras, L./Scaillet, O./Wermers, R. (2010): False Discoveries in Mutual Fund Performance: Measuring Luck in Estimated Alphas, in: The Journal of Finance, Vol. 65, p. 179–216.

Bär, M./Kempf, A./Ruenzi, S. (2011): Is a Team Different from the Sum of its Parts? Evidence from Mutual Fund Managers, in: Review of Finance, Vol. 15, p. 359–396.

Bechmann, K. L./Rangvid, J. (2007): Rating mutual funds: Construction and information content of an investor-cost based rating of Danish mutual funds, in: Journal of Empirical Finance, Vol. 14, p. 662–693.

Berk, J. B. /Green, R. C. (2004): Mutual fund flows and performance in rational markets, in: Journal of Political Economy, Vol. 112, p. 1269–1295.

Berzins, J./Liu, C. H./Trzcinka, C. (2013): Asset Management and Investment Banking, in: SSRN Electronic Journal, Journal of Financial Economics (JFE), Forthcoming.

Bessler, W./Drobetz, W./Zimmermann, H. (2009): Conditional performance evaluation for German equity mutual funds, in: The European Journal of Finance, Vol. 15, p. 287–316.

Blake, C. R./Morey, M. R. (2000): Morningstar ratings and mutual fund performance, in: Journal of Financial and Quantitative Analysis, Vol. 35, p. 451–483.

Bodson, L./Cavenaile, L./Sougné, D. (2013): A global approach to mutual funds market timing ability, in: Journal of Empirical Finance, Vol. 20, p. 96–101.

Bogle, J. C. (2010): The Challenge to Mutual Fund Stewardship, in: Haslem, John A. (2010): Mutual funds. Portfolio structures, analysis, management, and stewardship, Hoboken, NJ, p. 283-304.

Bollenn, N. P. (2007): Mutual Fund Attributes and Investor Behavior., in: Journal of International Financial Markets, Institutions and Money, Vol. 42, p. 683–708.

Brown, S. J./Goetzmann, W. N. (1995): Performance persistence, in: Journal of Finance, Vol. 50, p. 679–698.

Brown, K. C./Harlow, W. V./Strakes, L. T. (1996): Of Tournaments and Temptations: An Analysis of Managerial Incentives in the Mutual Fund Industry, in: Journal of Applied Finance, Vol. 51, p. 85–110.

Butler, A. W./Gurun, U. G. (2012): Educational Networks, Mutual Fund Voting Patterns, and CEO Compensation, in: Review of Financial Studies, Vol. 25, p. 2533–2562.

Carhart, M. M. (1997): On persistence in mutual fund performance, in: Journal of Finance, Vol. 52, p. 57–82.

Carhart, M. M./Kaniel, R./Musto, D. K./Reed, A. V. (2002): Leaning for the tape: Evidence from gaming behavior in equity mutual funds, in: The Journal of Finance, Vol. 57, p. 661–693.

67

Casarin, R./Lazzarin, M./Pelizzon, L./Sartore, D. (2005): Relative benchmark rating and persistence analysis: Evidence from Italian equity funds, in: The European Journal of Finance, Vol. 11, p. 297–308.

Celati, L. (2004): The dark side of risk management: How people frame decisions in financial markets, London.

Chen, J./Hong, H./Huang, M. /Kubik, J. D. (2004): Does fund size erode mutual fund performance?: The role of liquidity and organization, in: The American Economic Review, Vol. 94, p. 1276–1302.

Chen, C. R. /Huang, Y. (2011): Mutual Fund Governance and Performance: A Quantile Regression Analysis of Morningstar's Stewardship Grade, in: Corporate Governance: An International Review, Vol. 19, p. 311–333.

Chevalier, J. A./Ellison, G. (1997): Risk taking by mutual funds as a response to incentives, in: The journal of political economy, Vol. 105, p. 1167–1200.

Chevalier, J./Ellison, G. (1999a): Are some mutual fund managers better than others?: Cross-sectional patterns in behavior and performance, in: The Journal of Finance, Vol. 54, p. 875–899.

Chevalier, J./Ellison, G. (1999b): Career Concerns of Mutual Fund Managers, in: The Quarterly Journal of Economics, Vol. 114, p. 389–432.

Chou, J./Ng, L./Wang, Q. (2011): Are better governed funds better monitors?, in: Journal of Corporate Finance, Vol. 17, p. 1254–1271.

Christoffersen, S. E. K./Musto D. K. (2002): Demand Curves and the Pricing of Money Management, in: Review of Financial Studies, Vol. 15, p. 1499–1524.

Chung, K. H./Zhang, H. (2011): Corporate Governance and Institutional Ownership, in: Journal of Financial and Quantitative Analysis, Vol. 46, p. 247–273.

Ciccotello, Conrad S. (2010): The Nature of Mutual Funds, in: Haslem, John A. (2010): Mutual funds. Portfolio structures, analysis, management, and stewardship, Hoboken, NJ, p. 3-15.

Choi, J. J./Laibson, D./Madrian, B. C. (2010): Why Does the Law of One Price Fail? An Experiment on Index Mutual Funds, in: Review of Financial Studies, Vol. 23, p. 1405–1432.

Cici, G. (2012): The Prevalence of the Disposition Effect in Mutual Funds' Trades, in: Journal of Financial and Quantitative Analysis, Vol. 47, p. 795–820.

Cici, G./Gibson, S./Moussawi, R. (2010): Mutual fund performance when parent firms simultaneously manage hedge funds, in: Journal of Financial Intermediation, Vol. 19, p. 169–187.

Cremers, M./Driessen, J./Maenhout, P./Weinbaum, D. (2009): Does Skin in the Game Matter? Director Incentives and Governance in the Mutual Fund Industry, in: Journal of Financial and Quantitative Analysis, Vol. 44, p. 1345.

Cremers, K. J. M./Petajisto, A. (2009): How Active Is Your Fund Manager? A New Measure That Predicts Performance, in: Review of Financial Studies, Vol. 22, p. 3329-3365.

Curtis, Q./Morley, J. (2012): An Empirical Study of Mutual Fund Excessive Fee Litigation: Do the Merits Matter?, in: Journal of Law, Economics, and Organization.

Davis, J. L./Payne, G. T./McMahan, G. C. (2007): A Few Bad Apples? Scandalous Behavior of Mutual Fund Managers, in: Journal of Business Ethics, Vol. 76, p. 319-334.

Del Guercio, D. D./Tkac, P. A. (2001): Star power: The effect of Morningstar ratings on mutual fund flows, in: Working Paper Series (Federal Reserve Bank of Atlanta), Vol. 2001,15.

Del Guercio, D./Tkac, P. A. (2008): Star Power: The Effect of Morningstar Ratings on Mutual Fund Flow, in: Journal of Financial and Quantitative Analysis, Vol. 43, p. 907-936.

Denis, D. J./Denis, D. K. (1995): Performance Changes Following Top Management Dismissals, in: Journal of Finance, Vol. 50, p. 1029–1057.

Deutsche Asset & Wealth Management (2013): Exchange Traded Funds, on the internet: http://www.etf.db.com/DE/DEU/ETF/LU0274211480/DBX1DA/DAX%C2% AE_UCI TS_ETF.html, query: 06/09/2013, 8:30 p.m..

Deutsche Börse AG (2013): facts & figures Exchange Traded Funds, on the internet: http://xetra.com/INTERNET/EXCHANGE/zpd.nsf/KIR+Web+Publikationen/CPOL-947C8C/$FILE/XTF_Q3_2012_de.pdf?OpenElement, query: 03/20/2013, 8:30 p.m..

Ding, B. (2006): Mutual Fund Mergers: A Long-Term Analysis, in: SSRN Electronic Journal.

Ding, B./Wermers, R. R. (2012): Mutual Fund Performance and Governance Structure: The Role of Portfolio Managers and Boards of Directors, in: SSRN Electronic Journal.

Elton, E. J./Gruber, M. J./Blake, C. R. (2003): Incentive Fees and Mutual Funds, in: The Journal of Finance, Vol. 58, p. 779–804.

Evans, A. L. (2008): Portfolio manager ownership and mutual fund performance, in: Financial management, Vol. 37, p. 513–534.

Evans, R. B./Fahlenbrach, R. (2012): Institutional Investors and Mutual Fund Governance: Evidence from Retail-Institutional Fund Twins, in: Review of Financial Studies, Vol. 25, p. 3530–3571.

Fama, E. F. /French, K. R. (2010): Luck versus Skill in the Cross-Section of Mutual Fund Returns, in: The Journal of Finance, Vol. 65, p. 1915–1947.

Ferreira, M. A./Keswani, A./Miguel, A. F. /Ramos, S. B. (2013): The Determinants of Mutual Fund Performance: A Cross-Country Study, in: Review of Finance, Vol. 17, p. 483–525.

Ferris, S. P./Yan, X. (2009): Agency costs, governance, and organizational forms: Evidence from the mutual fund industry, in: Journal of Banking & Finance, Vol. 33, p. 619–626.

Ferson, W. E./Schadt, R. W. (1996): Measuring fund strategy and performance in changing economic conditions, in: Journal of Finance, Vol. 51, p. 425–461.

Fich, E. M./Shivdasani, A. (2006): Are Busy Boards Effective Monitors?, in: Journal of Finance, Vol. 61, p. 689–724.

Frank, M. M./Poterba, J. M./Shackelford, D. A./Shoven, J. B. (2004): Copycat Funds: Information Disclosure Regulation and the Returns to Active Management in the Mutual Fund Industry*, in: Journal of Law and Economics, Vol. 47, p. 515–541.

Fu, R./Wedge, L. (2011): Managerial ownership and the disposition effect, in: Journal of Banking & Finance, Vol. 35, p. 2407–2417.

Füss, R./Hille, J./Rindler, P./Schmidt, J./Schmidt, M. (2010): From rising stars and falling angels: On the relationship between the performance and ratings of German mutual funds, in: The Journal of Wealth Management, Vol. 13, p. 75–90.

Gaspar, J.-M./Massa, M./Matos, P. (2006): Favoritism in Mutual Fund Families? Evidence on Strategic Cross-Fund Subsidization, in: Journal of Finance, Vol. 61, p. 73-104.

Gerrans, P. (2006): Morningstar ratings and future performance, in: Accounting and Finance, Vol. 46, p. 605–628.

Gil-Bazo, J./Ruiz-Verdú, P. (2008): When cheaper is better: Fee determination in the market for equity mutual funds, in: Journal of Economic Behavior & Organization, Vol. 67, p. 871–885.

Gil-Bazo, J./Ruiz-Verdú, P. (2009): The Relation between Price and Performance in the Mutual Fund Industry, in: Journal of Finance, Vol. 64, p. 2153–2183.

Golec, J. (2003): Regulation and the Rise in Asset-Based Mutual Fund Fees, in: Journal of Financial Research, Vol. 26, p. 19–30.

Golez, B./Marin, J. M. (2012): Price Support by Bank-Affiliated Mutual Funds, in: SSRN Electronic Journal.

Gottesman, A./Morey, M. (2012): Mutual fund corporate culture and performance, in: Review of Financial Economics, Vol. 21, p. 69–81.

Hao, Q./Yan, X. (2012): The Performance of Investment Bank-Affiliated Mutual Funds: Conflicts of Interest or Informational Advantage?, in: Journal of Financial and Quantitative Analysis, Vol. 47, p. 537–565.

Heidorn, T./Winker, M,/Löw, C. (2010): Funktionsweise und Replikationsstil europäischer Exchange Traded Funds auf Aktienindices, in: Frankfurt School – Working Paper Series No. 139

Hendricks, D./Patel, J./Zeckhauser, R. J. (1993): Hot hands in mutual funds: Short-run persistence of relative performance, 1974 - 1988, in: Journal of Finance, p. 93–130.

Hereil, P./Mitaine, P./Moussavi, N./Roncalli, T. (2010): Mutual Fund Ratings and Performance Persistence, in: SSRN Electronic Journal.

Houge, T./Wellman, J. (2006): The Use and Abuse of Mutual Fund Expenses, in: Journal of Business Ethics, Vol. 70, p. 23–32.

Huang, J. C./Guedj, I. (2009): Are ETFs Replacing Index Mutual Funds?, in: SSRN Electronic Journal.

Huang, J./Sialm, C./Zhang, H. (2011): Risk Shifting and Mutual Fund Performance, in: Review of Financial Studies, Vol. 24, p. 2575–2616.

Iannotta, G./Navone, M. (2012): The cross-section of mutual fund fee dispersion, in: Journal of Banking & Finance, Vol. 36, p. 846–856.

ICI (2013): Investment Company Fact Book A Review of Trends and Activity in the U.S. Investment Company Industry, 53st ed., on the internet: http://www .ici.org/pdf /2013_factbook.pdf, query: 18/05/2013, 5:30 p.m..

Jank, S. (2010): Are there disadvantaged clienteles in mutual funds?, Frankfurt am Main.

Jank, S/Wedow, M. (2010): Purchase and redemption decisions of mutual fund investors and the role of fund families, Frankfurt am Main.

Jensen, M. C. (1968): The Performance of Mutual Funds in the Period 1945-1964, in: The Journal of Finance, Vol. 23, p. 389–419.

Tversky, A./Kahneman, D. (1974): Judgment under Uncertainty: Heuristics and Biases: Biases in judgments reversal some heuristics of thinking under uncertainty., in: Science, New Series, Vol. 185, p. 1124–1131.

Kahneman, D./Tversky, A. (1979): Prospect theory: An analysis of decision under risk, in: Econometrica: Journal of the Econometric Society, Vol. 47, p. 263–291.

Karagiannidis, I. (2010): Management team structure and mutual fund performance, in: Journal of International Financial Markets, Institutions and Money, Vol. 20, p. 197–211.

Kerr, N. L. (1992): Group decision making at a multialternative task: Extremity, interfaction distance, pluralities, and issue importance, in: Organizational Behavior and Human Decision Processes, Vol. 52, p. 64–95.

Khorana, A. (2001): Performance changes following top management turnover: Evidence from open-end mutual funds, in: Journal of Financial and Quantitative Analysis, Vol. 36, p. 371–393.

Khorana, A./Servaes, H./Tufano, P. (2007): Mutual Fund Fees Around the World, in: Review of Financial Studies, Vol. 22, p. 1279–1310.

Khorana, A./Tufano, P./Wedge, L. (2007a): Board structure, mergers, and shareholder wealth: A study of the mutual fund industry, in: Journal of financial economics, Vol. 85, p. 571–598.

Khorana, A./Servaes, H./Wedge, L. (2007b): Portfolio manager ownership and fund performance, in: Journal of financial economics, Vol. 85, p. 179–204.

Knuutila, M./Puttonen, V./Smythe, T. (2007): The effect of distribution channels on mutual fund flows, in: Journal of Financial Services Marketing, Vol. 12, p. 88–96.

Korkeamaki, T. P./Smythe, T. I. (2004): Effects of Market Segmentation and Bank Concentration on Mutual Fund Expenses and Returns: Evidence from Finland, in: European Financial Management, Vol. 10, p. 413–438.

Kosowski, R./Timmermann, A./Wermers, R./White, H. A. (2006): Can Mutual Fund "Stars" Really Pick Stocks? New Evidence from a Bootstrap Analysis, in: The Journal of Finance, Vol. 61, p. 2551–2595.

Kräussl, R./Sandelowsky, R. (2007): The Predictive Performance of Morningstar's Mutual Fund Ratings, in: SSRN Electronic Journal.

Kuhnen, C. M. (2005): Dynamic Contracting in the Mutual Fund Industry, in: SSRN Electronic Journal.

Kuhnen, C. M. (2009): Business Networks, Corporate Governance, and Contracting in the Mutual Fund Industry, in: Journal of Finance, Vol. 64, p. 2185–2220.

Li, H./Zhang, X./Zhao, R. (2011): Investing in Talents: Manager Characteristics and Hedge Fund Performances, in: Journal of Financial and Quantitative Analysis, Vol. 46, p. 59–82.

Lisi, F./Caporin, M. (2009): On the Role of Risk in the Morningstar Rating for Mutual Funds, in: SSRN Electronic Journal.

Madhur, S. (2005): Funds and Performance Fees Don't Mesh, in: Money Management Executive, Vol. 13, p. 5.

Malkiel, B. G. (2010): Efficient Markets and Mutual Fund Investing: The Advantages of Index Funds, in: Haslem, John A. (2010): Mutual funds. Portfolio structures, analysis, management, and stewardship, Hoboken, NJ, p. 119-137.

Mamudi,S (2009): Top Mutual Funds: Luck or Skill? New Study Questions'Active' Managers, in: The Wall Strett Journal, on the internet: http://online.wsj.com/article/SB10001424052748703735004574572293978523358.html,   query: 01/15/2013, 1:30 p.m..

Massa, M./Patgiri, R. (2007): Incentives and Mutual Fund Performance: Higher Performance or Just Higher Risk Taking?, in: Review of Financial Studies, Vol. 22, p. 1777–1815.

Massa, M./Rehman, Z. (2008): Information flows within financial conglomerates: Evidence from the banks–mutual funds relation, in: Journal of financial economics, Vol. 89, p. 288–306.

Massa, M./Reuter, J./Zitzewitz, E. (2010): When should firms share credit with employees? Evidence from anonymously managed mutual funds, in: Journal of Financial Economics, Vol. 95, p. 400–424.

Matsumura, E. M./Shin, J. Y. (2005): Corporate Governance Reform and CEO Compensation: Intended and Unintended Consequences, in: Journal of Business Ethics, Vol. 62, p. 101–113.

McCabe, P. E. (2009): The economics of the mutual fund trading scandal, in: Finance and Economics Discussion Series Divisions of Research & Statistics and Monetary Affairs Federal Reserve Board, Washington, D.C.,Vol. 2009,06.

Mehran, H./Stulz, R. M. (2007): The economics of conflicts of interest in financial institutions, in: Journal of Financial Economics, Vol. 85, p. 267–296.

Meier, I./Schaumburg, E. (2006): Do Funds Window Dress? Evidence for U.S. Domestic Equity Mutual Funds, in: Working Paper (HEC Montreal).

Meinhardt, C. (2011): Ratings and Performance of German Mutual Funds: A Comparison of Feri Trust, Euro Fondsnote and Finanztest, in: SSRN Electronic Journal.

Morningstar Inc.(2006): Das Morningstar Rating, on the internet: http://corporate .morningstar.com/de/documents/methodologydocuments/factsheets/de_morningstarratin gforfunds_factsheet.pdf, query: 03/15/2013, 1:30 p.m..

Morningstar Inc.(2010a): The Morningstar Rating for Funds, on the internet: http://corporate.morningstar.com/us/documents/methodologydocuments/factsheets/mor ningstarratingforfunds_factsheet.pdf, query: 03/15/2013, 1:30 p.m..

Morningstar Inc.(2010b): The Morningstar Stewardship Grade for Funds, on the internet: http://corporate.morningstar.com/us/documents/stewardshipgradefunds/Stew GradeMethodology_06-18-07.pdf, query: 03/15/2013, 2:30 p.m..

Nanda, V. K./Wang, Z. J./Zheng, L. (2009): The ABCs of mutual funds: On the introduction of multiple share classes, in: Journal of Financial Intermediation, Vol. 18, p. 329–361.

Nohel, T./Wang, Z. J./Zheng, L. (2010): Side-by-Side Management of Hedge Funds and Mutual Funds, in: Review of Financial Studies, Vol. 23, p. 2342–2373.

Palomino, F./Uhlig, H. (2007): Should smart investors buy funds with high past returns?, in: Review of Finance, Vol. 11, p. 51–70.

Phillips, D./ Kaplan, P. D. (2010): The Morningstar Approach to Mutual Fund Analysis-Part I, in: Haslem, John A. (2010): Mutual funds. Portfolio structures, analysis, management, and stewardship, Hoboken, NJ, p. 153-174.

Pollet, J. M./Wilson, M. (2008): How does size affect mutual fund behavior?, in: Journal of Finance, Vol. 63, p. 2941–2969.

Qian, M. (2011): Is "voting with your feet" an effective mutual fund governance mechanism?, in: Journal of Corporate Finance, Vol. 17, p. 45–61.

Qiu, J. (2003): Termination Risk, Multiple Managers and Mutual Fund Tournaments, in: Review of Finance, Vol. 7, p. 161–190.

Ritter, J. R./Zhang, D. (2007): Affiliated mutual funds and the allocation of initial public offerings, in: Journal of Financial Economics, Vol. 86, p. 337–368.

Russel, P. S. (2006): Do the Stars Foretell the Future?: The Performance of Morning Star Ratings, in: Journal of American Academy of Business, Vol. 10.

Sah, R. K./Stiglitz, J. E. (1988): Committees, hierarchies and polyarchies, in: The Economic Journal.

Schnatterly, K. (2003): Increasing firm value through detection and prevention of white-collar crime, in: Strategic Management Journal, Vol. 24, p. 587–614.

SEC (1999): Role of Independent Directors of Investment Companies, on the internet: http://www.sec.gov/rules/proposed/34-42007.htm, query: 05/25/2013, 10:30 p.m..

Shefrin, H./Statman, M. (1985): The disposition to sell winners too early and ride losers too long:: Theory and evidence, in: Journal of Finance, Vol. 40, p. 777–790.

Sharpe, W. F. (1998): Morningstar's Risk-Adjusted Ratings, in: Financial Analysts Journal, Vol. 54, p. 21–33.

Sirri, E. R./Tufano, P. (1998): Costly Search and Mutual Fund Flows;, in: Journal of Finance, Vol. 53, p. 1589–1622.

Smith, D. M. (2010a): The Economic of Mutual Funds, in: Haslem, John A. (2010): Mutual funds. Portfolio structures, analysis, management, and stewardship, Hoboken, NJ, p. 33-49.

Smith, D. M. (2010b): Mutual Fund Fees and Expenses, in: Haslem, John A. (2010): Mutual funds. Portfolio structures, analysis, management, and stewardship, Hoboken, NJ, p. 51-73.

Sørensen, J. B. (2002): The Strength of Corporate Culture and the Reliability of Firm Performance, in: Administrative Science Quarterly, Vol. 47, p. 70–91.

Terraza, V./Toque, C. (2009): The predictive power of fund ratings with a novel approach using uncertainty measures to analyzing risk, in: Decisions in Economics and Finance, Vol. 32, p. 149–160.

Tower, E./Zheng, W. (2008): Ranking mutual fund families: Minimum expenses and maximum loads as markers for moral turpitude, in: International Review of Economics, Vol. 55, p. 315–350.

Tversky, A./Kahneman, D. (1992): Advances in prospect theory: Cumulative representation of uncertainty, in: Journal of Risk and Uncertainty Vol. 5, p. 297–323.

Yan, X. ((2008): Liquidity, Investment Style, and the Relation between Fund Size and Fund Performance., in: Journal of Financial and Quantitative Analysis, Vol. 43, p. 741-767.

Zhao, X. (2005): Exit decisions in the US mutual fund industry, in: Journal of Business, Vol. 78, p. 1365–1402.